AROUND THE WORLD THROUGH HOLIDAYS

AROUND THE WORLD THROUGH HOLIDAYS

Cross Curricular Readers Theatre

Written and Illustrated by

Carol Peterson

Teacher Ideas Press, an imprint of Libraries Unlimited
Westport, Connecticut · London

Library of Congress Cataloging-in-Publication Data

Peterson, Carol, 1953–
    Around the world through holidays : cross curricular readers theatre/
written and illustrated by Carol Peterson.
      p. cm.
    Includes bibliographical references and index.
    ISBN 1-59469-013-8 (pbk. : alk. paper)
    1. Holidays—Cross-cultural studies—Juvenile literature. 2. Children's
plays—Cross-cultural studies—Juvenile literature. I. Title.
  GT3933.P48 2006
  394.26—dc22   2005030820

British Library Cataloguing in Publication Data is available.

Library of Congress Catalog Card Number: 2005030820
ISBN 1-59469-013-8

First published in 2006

Libraries Unlimited/Teacher Ideas Press, 88 Post Road West, Westport, CT 06881
A Member of the Greenwood Publishing Group, Inc.
www.lu.com

Printed in the United States of America

The paper used in this book complies with the
Permanent Paper Standard issued by the National
Information Standards Organization (Z39.48–1984).

10 9 8 7 6 5 4 3 2 1

The publisher has done its best to make sure the instructions and/or recipes in
this book are correct. However, users should apply judgment and experience
when preparing recipes, especially parents and teachers working with young
people. The publisher accepts no responsibility for the outcome of any recipe
included in this volume.

This book is dedicated to my terrific husband, Jim

and my two great kids, Doug and Nicole.

It was written with gratitude for all the children of the world

and for God, who loves us all.

Contents

Introduction   **1**
  What is Readers Theatre?   1
    Nontheatrical Reading   1
    Theatrical Performance Reading   1
  How to Use this Resource   2
  Tips for Success   2
    Roles   2
    Rehearsal   3
    Performance   3
    Costumes, Props, and Characterization   3
    Readers Theatre Terms   3

HOLIDAY READERS THEATRE

January—New Year (USA, China, South Korea, Venezuela, Greece, Australia, Scotland)   **7**
  Background   7
  Readers Theatre Script—*Happy New Year!*   7
  Follow-Up Activities   21
    Where in the World Am I? (Geography)   21
    Make a Flag of Scotland (Math, Art)   22
    National Anthem of Australia (Literacy, Music)   23
    Currency Conversion (Math)   23
  Have a New Year Celebration   24
    Seesaw (Science)   24
    Chinese Paper Cutting (Math, Art)   24
    Korean Yut Game (Math)   25
    Auld Lang Syne (Literacy, Music)   27
  Suggestions for Further Activities   27

February—Fastelavn (Denmark)   **29**
  Background   29
  Readers Theatre Script—*Tilting the Barrel*   29

Follow-Up Activities   37
    Where in the World Am I? (Geography)   37
    Make a Flag of Denmark (Math, Art)   37
    National Anthem of Denmark (Literacy, Music, Geography, Social Studies)   38
    Currency Conversion (Math)   39
Have a Fastelavn Celebration   39
    Ladyfingers Recipe (Math)   39
    Tilting the Barrel (Activity, Art, Physical Education)   40
    Lenten Branches (Art, Science)   40
    Calculate the Height of a Tree (Math)   40
    Danish Folk Dance (Physical Education)   42
    Golden Crowns (Art, Math)   44
    Black Cats (History, Science, Art)   45
Suggestions for Further Activities   45

March—Happy St. Patrick's Day (Ireland)   47
Background   47
Readers Theatre Script—*Kidnapped!*   47
Follow-Up Activities   55
    Where in the World Am I? (Geography)   55
    Make a Flag of Ireland (Math, Art)   55
    National Anthem of Ireland (Literacy, Music)   56
    Currency Conversion (Math)   57
Have a St. Patrick's Day Celebration   57
    Trifle (Math)   57
    Paper Chains (Math, Art)   58
    Shamrocks (Science, Art)   58
    Leprechaun Footprints (Language Arts, Art)   58
    Celtic Designs (Math, Art)   59
    Limericks (Language Arts, Literacy, Geography, History, Math)   60
    Brainstorming Saints (Literacy)   61
Suggestions for Further Activities   61

April—Passover (Israel)   62
Background   62
Readers Theatre Script—*Escape to Freedom*   62
Follow-Up Activities   75
    Where in the World Am I? (Geography)   75
    Make a Flag of Israel (Math, Art)   75
    National Anthem of Israel (Literacy, Geography, Music)   77
    Currency Conversion (Math)   77
Have a Passover Celebration   77
    Charoset Recipe (Math)   78
    Matzo Bread Recipe (Math)   78
    Frogs (Math, Art)   79
    Timeline (Math, History)   85
Suggestions for Further Activities   85

May—May Day (England, Scotland, France, Italy, Germany, Russia, USA)   86
  Background   86
  Readers Theatre Script—*The Merry Month of May*   86
  Follow-Up Activities   96
    Where in the World Am I? (Geography)   96
    Make a Flag of France (Math, Art)   96
    National Anthem of Germany (Literacy, Music)   97
    Currency Conversion (Math)   98
  Have a May Day Celebration   98
    Treacle Parkin Recipe (Math)   98
    Bannock Recipe (Math)   99
    May Dance (Math, Physical Education, Music)   100
    May Baskets (Math, Art, Community Service)   100
    Springy Poetry (Language Arts)   100
    Planting Flowers (Science)   101
  Suggestions for Further Activities   101

June—Dragon Boat Festival (China)   102
  Background   102
  Readers Theatre Script—*Searching for Chu Yuan*   102
  Follow-Up Activities   110
    Where in the World Am I? (Geography)   110
    Make a Flag of China (Math, Art)   110
    National Anthem of China (Literacy, Music)   112
    Currency Conversion (Math)   112
  Have a Dragon Boat Celebration   112
    Rice Ball Recipe (Math)   112
    Traditional Zongzi Recipe (Science, Math)   113
    Dragon Head (Art)   114
    Xiangbao Pouches (Science, Art)   115
  Suggestions for Further Activities   116

July—Independence Day (United States)   117
  Background   117
  Readers Theatre Script—*Freedom Isn't Free*   117
  The Declaration of Independence (Literacy)   127
  Follow-Up Activities
    Where in the World Am I? (Geography)   127
    Make a Flag of Colonial America (Math, Art)   127
    National Anthem of the United States (Literacy, History, Music)   129
    Currency Conversion (Math)   130
  Have an Independence Day Celebration   130
    Johnnycakes Recipe (Math)   130
    Learn the Names of the Thirteen Colonies (Literacy, History)   131
    Dominoes (Math)   131
    Go Fly a Kite! (Math, Science, Art)   133
  Suggestions for Further Activities   134

August—Obon (Japan)   135

Background   135

Readers Theatre Script—*Until Next Year, Grandpa Sato*   135

Follow-Up Activities   144

    Where in the World Am I? (Geography)   144

    Make a Flag of Japan (Math, Art)   144

    National Anthem of Japan (Literacy, Music)   145

    Currency Conversion (Math)   145

Have an Obon Celebration   145

    Ramen Soup Recipe (Math)   146

    Paper Fans (Art, Math)   146

    Bon Odori Dance (Physical Education)   147

    Paper Lanterns (Art)   147

    Toro Nagashi Boats (Science, Art)   148

    Haiku (Literacy, Language Arts)   149

    Japanese Phrases (Literacy, Language Arts)   149

Suggestions for Further Activities   150

September—Homowo (Ghana)   151

Background   151

Readers Theatre Script—*Hooting at Hunger!*   151

Follow-Up Activities   159

    Where in the World Am I? (Geography)   159

    Make a Flag of Ghana (Math, Art)   159

    National Anthem of Ghana (Literacy, Music)   161

    Currency Conversion (Math)   161

Have a Homowo Celebration   162

    Yam Foofoo Recipe (Math)   162

    Hot Plantain Crisp Recipe (Math, Science)   162

    Hydroelectric Power (Geography, Science)   163

    Adinkra Cloth (Math, Science, Art)   164

    Play a Folk Game from Ghana (Physical Education)   165

Suggestions for Further Activities   165

October—Divali (India)   166

Background   166

Readers Theatre Script—*Festival of Lights*   166

Follow-Up Activities   175

    Where in the World Am I? (Geography)   175

    Make a Flag of India (Math, Art)   175

    National Anthem of India (Literacy, Geography, Music)   176

    Currency Conversion (Math)   177

Have a Divali Celebration   177

    Make a Divali Lamp (Art)   177

    Saris and Turbans (Costumes, Social Studies)   177

    Rangoli (Art, Social Studies)   179

Pachisi Game (Math)   179
Barfi Candy Recipe (Math)   181
Suggestions for Further Activities   181

November—Ramadan (Saudi Arabia, Kuwait)   182
Background   182
Readers Theatre Script—*The Five Pillars*   182
Follow-Up Activities   192
Where in the World Am I? (Geography)   192
Make a Flag of Kuwait (Math, Art)   192
National Anthem of Kuwait (Literacy, Music)   194
Currency Conversion (Math)   194
Have a Ramadan Celebration   194
Ma'amoul Cookie Recipe (Math)   194
Eid Greeting Cards (Language Arts, Art)   195
Helping the Community (Physical Education, Community Service)   196
Muslim Calendar (Math, Science, Literacy, Language Arts, Art)   196
Locating Mecca (Geography, Science)   197
Suggestions for Further Activities   198

December—Las Posadas (Mexico)   199
Background   199
Readers Theatre Script—*Outside the Inn*   199
Follow-Up Activities   208
Where in the World Am I? (Geography)   208
Make a Flag of Mexico (Math, Art)   208
National Anthem of Mexico (Literacy, Music)   210
Currency Conversion (Math)   211
Have a Las Posadas Celebration   211
Bizcochito Recipe (Math)   211
Faroles and Farolitos (Art)   212
Piñata (Math, Art)   213
Suggestions for Further Activities   215

SUPPLEMENTAL CHAPTERS

Timelines and Number Lines   219
Timelines   219
Make Your Own Timeline (Language Arts)   219
Number Lines   220
Make a Thermometer Chart (Science, Math)   220

Calendars   221
Our Solar Calendar   221
Lunar Calendars   222
Stars of Wonder (Science, Language Arts)   223

Latitude and Longitude   224
   Latitude   224
   Longitude   224
      Where in the World Are We? (Math, Geography)   225

Measurements and Metric Conversions   226
   Do It Yourself   226
      Measuring Capacity   226
      Measuring Weight   226
      Measuring Distance   227
      Measuring Area   227
      Measuring Temperature   227

Flags   228
   Flag Symbolism   228
   Parts of a Flag   228
      Vexing Vexillology (Art)   229

Appendix—Recommended Resources for Teachers and Students   230

Bibliography   232

Index   233

Introduction

Before you start any journey, you need to haul out your suitcase, toss in some clothes, and grab your ticket. As you begin your journey *Around the World Through Holidays,* this chapter will give you some things to tuck inside your Readers Theatre suitcase: a summary of Readers Theatre formats, information on how to use this resource, and tips to make each holiday a lively, educational success.

WHAT IS READERS THEATRE?

Readers Theatre is simply a form of play presented through oral reading. Readers Theatre is most typically used in two formats: nontheatrical reading and theatrical performance reading. No matter which format you choose, though, the parts are intended to be read—not memorized.

Nontheatrical Reading

In a nontheatrical setting students simply read scripts aloud as a group, and the scripts merely represent a reading resource. One way to read scripts is in **circle reading,** where all students read the various parts by taking turns around a circle. Each student reads one line, followed by the next student who reads the next line. In circle reading, no one student reads all of the lines of any one role. Scripts may also be used in **instant reading,** where students are assigned parts and the play is simply read once from their seats. Alternatively, students may be assigned parts, read through the script silently, and then read it through aloud once.

Theatrical Performance Reading

An alternate focus for Readers Theatre is theatrical performance. Here, roles are read standing in front of the classroom or on a stage. Performances might include simple costumes and props, rehearsal, stage direction, facial expression, gestures, and sound effects. Even in a performance setting, however, scripts are not memorized. The emphasis is to encourage literacy through *reading*.

Plays in a theatrical setting might be performed as **cooperative reading.** This format breaks a classroom into groups. Scripts are rehearsed individually by reading aloud, and then rehearsed once or twice as a group. Each group then performs the entire play to the others.

Plays may also be a **staged reading,** where a specific area of the classroom is selected as the "stage" or an actual stage is used, if available. Entrances and exits are included and rehearsed. Plays might then be presented to other classes in the same grade level or to other grade levels within the school.

Each script includes performance suggestions for props, action, gestures, and stage entrances and exits, for optional use in a theatrical performance format. If a nonperformance format is used, these suggestions can be ignored, or one student may be assigned to read them aloud.

HOW TO USE THIS RESOURCE

Around the World Through Holidays includes scripts for twelve plays that are adaptable for either nontheatrical or performance readings. Scripts introduce students to specific cultures by looking at holidays celebrated in those cultures. The book structure introduces holidays *chronologically through a calendar year*—one play per month—in a way that seeks to represent the world geographically.

Despite the chronological structure, the focus of the plays is not the calendar. Teachers should therefore not feel limited by a traditional school year. In other words, Obon may be celebrated during August in Japan, but students in America would still enjoy celebrating it in March if that is when their social studies curriculum introduces the country or culture of Japan.

In addition to a focus on literacy, each of the twelve holiday chapters includes four specific follow-up activities: a geography activity, a flag-making activity, lyrics to a country's national anthem, and a currency exchange activity. You will want to have a world atlas or large world map with enough topographical detail so students will be able to identify major cities and geographical features of the countries being studied. Each holiday chapter also includes ideas for a classroom holiday celebration, plus ideas for further follow-up activities. The variety of activities is meant to enhance students' cross-curricular experience—as well as the fun.

In addition to the twelve holiday chapters, further material, intended to be photocopied and read aloud by students is included in five supplementary chapters. They contain activities that can be used separately or along with the holiday chapters. These five chapters cover:

- ❖ Timelines and number lines
- ❖ Calendars
- ❖ Longitude and latitude
- ❖ Measurements and metric conversions
- ❖ Flags

TIPS FOR SUCCESS

Roles

The twelve scripts have varying numbers of parts. Each script includes two narrators. If there is a large number of students, consider having a set of different narrators for each scene. If the class size is small, or if students are divided into groups to present to each other, you may want to assign students more than one part. For example, if a play has roles for Villagers 1, 2, 3, and 4, one student might take the roles of both Villager 1 and Villager 3.

One way to introduce characters to the audience at the beginning of the play is to line the characters up facing the audience. Students then introduce themselves in turn saying, for example, "I am playing the part of Jose." Alternatively, each student can carry the script in a folder with the character's name printed on the front in large letters for the audience to see.

Rehearsal

Encourage students to follow along as others read. Have them rehearse their parts in pairs and help each other with words. For performance theatre, first practice the play seated in a circle a few times. Then have readers begin rehearsing the play with gestures, expression, and movement. Finally, rehearse the play in the staging area with entrances and exits, using proper stage directions. Don't worry too much about entrances and exits. If the stage area is small and there is no room for a "backstage," readers can enter the performance area by walking through or around the audience.

Performance

Photocopy scripts as needed. Make sure each reader has a script with the character's name highlighted. Encourage readers to speak loudly. Remind students that the more familiar with they are with the part, the more professional the performance will be (and the better their literacy and self confidence). Do not encourage memorization, however. This is **readers** theatre.

Instruct students to talk to the audience, rather than to each other, to help project their voices and make the audience feel a part of the play. Instruct students to hold scripts away from their faces, so their facial expressions can be seen and their words are not muffled.

Encourage eye contact between the reader and the audience. Although the reader will have to look down at the script from time to time, encourage the readers to focus on a point at the back of the room, slightly above the audience. When characters speak to each other, they should continue to speak to that point above the audience, as if that is the location of the other character.

Costumes, Props, and Characterization

There are suggestions for costumes and props for each script. Keep in mind, however, that readers will need one hand free to hold the script, so costumes and props should be simple.

During rehearsal, discuss the culture, time in history, and the characters—what the character is feeling or thinking and how that changes throughout the story. Discuss how the reader can show those things to the audience by changing voice, posture, and movements.

Readers Theatre Terms

You may want to introduce students to the following theatrical terms, especially if using the performance format of Readers Theatre.

- ❖ Backstage and Offstage—area that is not the stage
- ❖ Cast—people reading the play
- ❖ Downstage—the portion of the stage in front of the reader
- ❖ Dress rehearsal—practicing the play as it will be performed, using costumes and props
- ❖ Narrator—person who explains the action or setting
- ❖ Performance—reading the script to an audience

- ❖ Readers—students who provide the action and the drama
- ❖ Rehearsal—practicing the play
- ❖ Script—the play being read
- ❖ Stage—the area where the play is read
- ❖ Stage left—the portion of the stage to the reader's left
- ❖ Stage right—the portion of the stage to the reader's right
- ❖ Upstage—the portion of the stage behind the reader

Now that your suitcase is packed, you're ready to go. Have a great time on your journey *Around the World Through Holidays*!

HOLIDAY READERS THEATRE

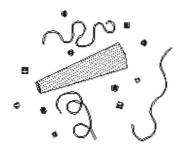

January—New Year

(USA, China, South Korea, Venezuela, Greece, Australia, Scotland)

BACKGROUND

Ancient people celebrated the beginning of a new year at different times. Some celebrated at harvest time because harvest meant a time of plenty. Others celebrated during spring, when nature renewed itself. In 153 BC the Romans set the beginning of the year in January, because that was when senators began their new government. Our present calendar had its origins in the Roman one. (See the chapter entitled **Calendars.**)

READERS THEATRE SCRIPT—HAPPY NEW YEAR!

Suggested Costumes and Props

- ❖ Bag of noisemakers to give 1 or 2 to the kids in each country (Scenes 2, 3, 5, 6, 7, 8)
- ❖ Two chairs to represent the Super Speedy Shuttle (all scenes)
- ❖ Sheet or large cloth to cover Super Speedy Shuttle (Scene 1)
- ❖ Optional cardboard machine façade for the Super Speedy Shuttle (all scenes)
- ❖ Book (Scene 1—Super Speedy Shuttle instruction book)
- ❖ Sheet of paper (Scene 1)
- ❖ Empty toilet paper rolls tied with string to represent firecrackers (Scene 2)
- ❖ Packet of paper (Scene 2)

❖ Box, bag, or pouch representing the Yut game (Scene 3)

❖ Suitcases (Scene 5)

❖ Grapes—plastic or real (Scene 5)

❖ Beachwear, towels, picnic basket, lawn chair, sunglasses, etc. (Scene 6)

❖ Boomerang or cardboard replica (Scene 6)

❖ Piece of paper for song lyrics (Scene 8)

❖ Costumes from any of the countries visited

Characters

The following is a list of characters. Nonspeaking roles may include one or more students who make machine sounds. Additional students may sing "Auld Lang Syne."

- NARRATOR 1
- NARRATOR 2
- JOSH
- SELENA
- CHINESE BOY
- CHINESE GIRL
- KOREAN BOY
- KOREAN GIRL

- VENEZUELAN BOY
- VENEZUELAN GIRL
- AUSTRALIAN BOY
- AUSTRALIAN GIRL
- GREEK BOY
- GREEK GIRL
- SCOTTISH BOY
- SCOTTISH GIRL

Presentation Suggestions

This play includes 8 scenes. Narrator 1, Narrator 2, Josh, and Selena will be onstage at all times. As they "land" in each country, the children from that country may walk onstage from stage left or stage right and exit at the end of that scene. Consider decorating the back of the stage with a flag from each of the countries Josh and Selena visit by having a student carry the new flag onstage and replace it at each scene change. The **SETTING** at the beginning of each scene is to assist characters and is not intended to be read. Performance suggestions (gestures, movements, facial expressions) and pronunciation helps are in brackets.

Happy New Year!

Scene 1—In the Attic

SETTING: An attic in an American home. Onstage are Narrator 1, Narrator 2, Josh, and Selena.

NARRATOR 1:	It is December 31. Josh and Selena are in the attic looking for decorations for their New Year party.
NARRATOR 2:	They find a bag of noisemakers and a sheet covering something big.
JOSH:	I wonder what's under here.
	[Josh pulls off a sheet covering 2 chairs that represent the Super Speedy Shuttle.]
SELENA:	It's a machine.
JOSH:	There's a book that goes with it.
SELENA:	[reading over his shoulder] "Super Speedy Shuttle."
JOSH:	[reading] "Travel the world at the speed of light."
SELENA:	Hey, you know what would be cool?
JOSH:	What?
SELENA:	To find out how kids in other countries celebrate the New Year!
JOSH:	Let's get in!
NARRATOR 1:	Josh and Selena sit in the machine.
SELENA:	How does it work?
NARRATOR 2:	Josh reads the directions.
JOSH:	[reading directions] "Directions for a world tour."
SELENA:	That sounds perfect! What do we do?
JOSH:	It says "Enter latitude."
SELENA:	Oh! Well, pick a number.
JOSH:	Okay—39.55. [pronounced thirty-nine point fifty-five]
SELENA:	Why is it asking if we want N or S?

From *Around the World Through Holidays: Cross Curricular Readers Theatre* written and illustrated by Carol Peterson. Westport, CT: Teacher Ideas Press/Libraries Unlimited. Copyright © 2006.

JOSH:	I don't know.
SELENA:	Just push N. [Josh pushes buttons]
NARRATOR 1:	Josh pushes buttons but nothing happens.
JOSH:	[reading] Now it asks for a longitude number.
SELENA:	How about 116.20?
	[pronounced one hundred sixteen point twenty]
	[Selena pushes buttons]
NARRATOR 2:	Selena pushes buttons, but still nothing happens.
JOSH:	Now it's asking if I want E or W.
SELENA:	Try E.
JOSH:	It's still not doing anything.
SELENA:	Maybe it's like a computer where you have to hit "enter."
JOSH:	[pushes button] Okay, I'll hit the "return" key.
	[offstage sound of machine noises]
	[Josh and Selena shake in their chairs to suggest the machine's engine vibrations]
NARRATOR 1:	The Super Speedy Shuttle takes off!
NARRATOR 1:	After a whoosh and a bang, it stops!
	[Josh and Selena stop shaking; sound of machine noises stops]

Scene 2—China

SETTING: Onstage are Josh, Selena, Narrator 1, and Narrator 2. Entering from stage left or right are a Chinese boy and girl. The location is Beijing, China. [pronounced bay-ZHING]

NARRATOR 1:	Josh and Selena have landed…
NARRATOR 2:	…in Beijing, the capital city of China.
JOSH:	I've seen pictures of this place. We're in China.
SELENA:	[looking at map] Oh, I get it! The numbers of the latitude and longitude…
JOSH:	[looking at the map] …are the location of this city!
	[Josh and Selena climb out of the machine]
NARRATOR 1:	Just then two Chinese kids walk by.

JOSH:	Happy New Year!
CHINESE GIRL:	You're a month too early for the New Year.
JOSH:	But tomorrow is January 1st.
CHINESE BOY:	Chinese New Year isn't January 1st.
SELENA:	When is it?
CHINESE GIRL:	It's at the end of January or early February…
CHINESE BOY:	…depending on the moon. Can you come back then?
SELENA:	No, we're looking for ideas to celebrate the New Year now.
JOSH:	How do you celebrate in China?
CHINESE GIRL:	We get rid of evil spirits.
SELENA:	How?
CHINESE BOY:	We light firecrackers to scare them away. You can buy some down the street.
JOSH:	That sounds like fun. But we don't want firecrackers in our travel machine. It might explode!
SELENA:	What else do you do?
CHINESE GIRL:	We cut out paper pictures and cover our windows to keep out evil spirits.
SELENA:	How lovely.
CHINESE BOY:	[handing them a packet] You can take our paper.
JOSH:	Thank you. Here is one of our noisemakers for you.
CHINESE GIRL:	Thank you.
SELENA:	How do you wish each other Happy New Year?
CHINESE BOY:	We say "GUNG HAY FAT CHOY."
CHINESE GIRL:	It means, "May you be prosperous."
JOSH & SELENA:	GUNG HAY FAT CHOY to you.
NARRATOR 1:	Josh and Selena climb back into the Super Speedy Shuttle.
NARRATOR 2:	Josh and Selena wave goodbye. [Chinese boy and girl exit]
SELENA:	Where shall we go next?
JOSH:	[looking at a map] Let's enter latitude 37.31 N [pronounced thirty-seven point thirty-one North].
SELENA:	[looking at the map] And longitude 126.58 E [pronounced one hundred twenty-six point fifty-eight East].

JOSH:	That should take us to Seoul, Korea.
	[pronounced SOLE, koh-REE-uh]
SELENA:	I hope they're celebrating the New Year.
	[Offstage machine noises]
	[Josh and Selena shake in their chairs]

Scene 3—South Korea

SETTING: Onstage are Josh, Selena, Narrator 1, and Narrator 2. Entering from stage left or right are a Korean boy and girl. The location is Seoul, Korea. [Josh and Selena stop shaking; sound of machine noises stops]

NARRATOR 1:	Josh and Selena land in Seoul.
NARRATOR 2:	Seoul is the capital city of South Korea.
NARRATOR 1:	They climb out of their Super Speedy Shuttle.
NARRATOR 2:	Two Korean children walk by.
JOSH:	Excuse me—Happy New Year!
KOREAN BOY:	Happy New Year to you, too!
KOREAN GIRL:	But the really big celebration called "Sol-nal" isn't now.
SELENA:	You celebrate the New Year twice?
KOREAN BOY:	Yes, once now when you do.
KOREAN GIRL:	And we also celebrate the Chinese New Year.
SELENA:	There are so many people out tonight.
KOREAN GIRL:	No one sleeps on New Year's Eve.
JOSH:	Because everyone is having parties?
KOREAN BOY:	No. If we fall asleep on New Year's Eve our eyebrows turn white.
SELENA:	What?
KOREAN GIRL:	That's what we believe.
JOSH:	Do you know anyone whose eyebrows turned white on New Year's Eve?
KOREAN BOY:	No—because everyone stays awake to make sure they don't!
SELENA:	Well, how do you celebrate the New Year?
KOREAN GIRL:	On Sol-nal we start the day with a special soup.

JOSH:	Soup for breakfast?
KOREAN BOY:	It's called Ttok-kuk.
	[pronounced TOCK-KUK]
SELENA:	What's in it?
KOREAN GIRL:	Beef broth and sliced rice cake.
KOREAN BOY:	By eating the bowl of soup you become a year older.
JOSH:	How does eating soup make you a year older?
KOREAN GIRL:	It's like your birthday cake.
KOREAN BOY:	We don't celebrate birthdays on the date we were born.
KOREAN GIRL:	Instead, everyone becomes a year older on the New Year.
SELENA:	So the rice cake in the soup IS your birthday cake.
KOREAN GIRL:	After the soup, then everyone bows.
KOREAN BOY:	It's called the jol. Let me show you how.
	[Korean boy kneels down and bows with hands on floor in front of him]
JOSH:	Why do you bow?
KOREAN GIRL:	To wish each other good luck, health, and long life.
KOREAN BOY:	Then the boys spin tops.
KOREAN GIRL:	And girls play on the seesaw.
SELENA:	We have a seesaw at school. It's a board you sit on and go up and down.
KOREAN GIRL:	You SIT on a seesaw? In Korea we STAND on the board and jump up and down.
JOSH:	Don't you fall off?
KOREAN GIRL:	Sometimes. That's what makes it fun.
SELENA:	Boys spin tops and girls seesaw. Is there anything you can do together?
KOREAN GIRL:	We play Yut!
JOSH:	What's Yut?
KOREAN BOY:	It's a board game.
KOREAN GIRL:	[hands Josh a package] Take our game and play it when you get home.
JOSH:	Thanks! We should go.
SELENA:	We're still looking for a country that celebrates the New Year when we do.
JOSH:	[handing a noisemaker to the Korean boy and girl]

	Here—take one of our noisemakers and think of us during Sol-nal.
KOREAN BOY:	Thanks!
KOREAN GIRL:	Don't forget the jol.
NARRATOR 1:	Everyone bows and the Korean boy and girl leave.
	[Korean boy and girl exit]
NARRATOR 2:	Josh and Selena climb back in their machine.
SELENA:	Paper cutting, games, birthday soup… New Year is fun!
JOSH:	But let's find someplace that only celebrates it now.

Scene 4—Back Inside the Super Speedy Shuttle

SETTING: Onstage are Josh, Selena, Narrator 1, and Narrator 2. The location is still Seoul, Korea—inside the Super Speedy Shuttle.

NARRATOR 1:	Josh and Selena look at the Super Speedy Shuttle instructions.
SELENA:	Where shall we go next? Egypt?
JOSH:	No, my friend Hassan says Muslims celebrate the New Year in March.
SELENA:	We could go to India. But my friend Amrit says they celebrate the New Year in October.
JOSH:	We could go to Israel. But my friend Daniel celebrates the Jewish New Year in October.
SELENA:	There must be someplace that celebrates the New Year now.
JOSH:	[pushes button] Let's try this one. Press 10.30 N.
	[pronounced ten point thirty North]
SELENA:	Now press 66.56 W.
	[pronounced sixty-six point fifty-six West]
JOSH:	[looking at map] We're off to Caracas, Venezuela!
	[pronounced kah-RAH-kus, ven-ez-WALE-ya]
NARRATOR 1:	But Josh and Selena just sit quietly.
NARRATOR 2:	Their Super Speedy Shuttle doesn't move.

SELENA: [pushes button] You forgot to push the "return" button.

NARRATOR 1: Now the Super Speedy Shuttle is working again.

NARRATOR 2: Off they go!

[Offstage machine noises]

[Josh and Selena shake in their chairs]

Scene 5—Venezuela

SETTING: Onstage are Narrator 1, Narrator 2, Josh, and Selena. Entering from stage left or right are a Venezuelan boy and girl. The location is Caracas, Venezuela.[Josh and Selena stop shaking; sound of machine noises stops]

NARRATOR 1: Josh and Selena exit their Super Speedy Shuttle.

NARRATOR 2: Two children walk by carrying suitcases.

JOSH: Happy New Year!

VENEZUELAN BOY: Happy New Year to you, too!

SELENA: Where are you going?

VENEZUELAN GIRL: We're not going anywhere right now.

JOSH: But you're carrying suitcases.

VENEZEUELAN BOY: Of course! They're empty.

VENEZUELAN GIRL: We're carrying them because we want to travel NEXT year.

SELENA: Why carry them now?

VENEZUELAN GIRL: It's a tradition.

VENEZUELAN BOY: Do you have your grapes for midnight?

JOSH: Why do we need grapes?

VENEZUELAN GIRL: You eat one grape for every chime when the clock strikes midnight.

SELENA: You eat twelve grapes at midnight?

VENEZUELAN BOY: Yes! You have to eat them fast for good luck!

VENEZUELAN GIRL: Here. Take some of mine.

NARRATOR 1: She hands some grapes to Josh and Selena.

JOSH:	[hands a noisemaker to the Venezuelan boy and girl]
	Thank you. We like to make noise to celebrate the New Year. Take one of our noisemakers.
VENEZUELAN GIRL:	Thank you. Do you have on your yellow underwear?
SELENA:	What?
VENEZUELAN BOY:	Yellow underwear brings good luck!
JOSH:	Thanks for the tip.
SELENA:	We'd better finish our trip if we need time to find yellow underwear.
JOSH:	Thanks for the grapes.
SELENA:	Happy New Year.
VENEZUELAN BOY and GIRL:	[waving] PRÓSPERO AÑO NUEVO to you, too!
	[pronounced PROS-peh-row AHN-yo new-EV-oh]
NARRATOR 1:	Josh and Selena climb back into their Super Speedy Shuttle.
JOSH:	Paper cutting, games, birthday soup, grapes, and yellow underwear.
SELENA:	Where to next?
NARRATOR 2:	Josh reads the map.
JOSH:	Push latitude 35.15 S; longitude 149.08 E—and push the "return" button.
	[pronounced thirty-five point fifteen South; one hundred forty-nine point zero eight East]
NARRATOR 1:	Selena checks the map.
SELENA:	We're heading south. Way south!
	[Offstage machine noises]
	[Josh and Selena shake in their chairs]

Scene 6—Australia

SETTING: Onstage are Narrator 1, Narrator 2, Josh, and Selena. Entering from stage left or right are an Australian boy and girl. The location is Canberra, Australia. [Josh and Selena stop shaking; sound of machine noises stops]

NARRATOR 2:	Josh and Selena arrive in Canberra.
NARRATOR 1:	Canberra is the capital city of Australia.

JOSH:	Where is everyone?
SELENA:	Maybe we missed the New Year. The weather is so hot!
NARRATOR 1:	An Australian boy and girl walk by in beach clothes.
	[Australian boy and girl enter stage left or stage right]
JOSH:	Excuse me. What day is it?
AUSTRALIAN BOY:	It's New Year's Eve, mate.
SELENA:	Where is everyone?
AUSTRALIAN GIRL:	At the beach, having a picnic.
JOSH:	They're at the beach in January?
AUSTRALIAN BOY:	Of course in January—it's summertime for us.
SELENA:	New Year in the summer time? What fun!
JOSH:	We're collecting ideas for how to celebrate the New Year.
SELENA:	A picnic is great anytime. Even if it's indoors in the winter!
AUSTRALIAN BOY:	Here—take our boomerang, and next time you have a picnic OUTDOORS, try throwing it.
SELENA:	[handing him a noisemaker] Thanks! And here's a noisemaker from us to you.
AUSTRALIAN GIRL:	Thanks. Happy New Year.
JOSH:	Happy New Year to you, too!
NARRATOR 2:	Josh and Selena climb back into their Super Speedy Shuttle.
SELENA:	Paper cutting, games, birthday soup, grape eating, yellow underwear, and picnics.
JOSH:	Enter latitude 37.58 N; longitude 23.46 E and press "return."
	[pronounced thirty-seven point fifty-eight North; twenty-three point forty-six East]
NARRATOR 2:	Josh and Selena's shuttle takes off again.
	[Offstage machine noises]
	[Josh and Selena shake in their chairs]

Scene 7—Greece

SETTING: Onstage are Narrator 1, Narrator 2, Josh, and Selena. Entering from stage left or right are a Greek boy and girl. The location is Athens, Greece. [Josh and Selena stop shaking; sound of machine noises stops]

NARRATOR 1: Josh and Selena climb out of the Super Speedy Shuttle.

NARRATOR 2: They have arrived in Athens, the capital city of Greece.

GREEK BOY: [waving] Happy St. Basil's day.

JOSH: St. Basil's day? Don't you celebrate the New Year?

GREEK GIRL: Yes, but we also celebrate St. Basil's day.

SELENA: Who was St. Basil?

GREEK BOY: He was a kind man who lived long ago and brought gifts to children.

GREEK GIRL: Children leave their shoes by the fireplace and in the morning they're filled with gifts.

JOSH: That sounds like Santa Claus at Christmas time.

SELENA: How else do you celebrate?

GREEK BOY: With cake.

JOSH: Birthday cake soup, like in Korea?

GREEK GIRL: No, it's a special New Year cake.

SELENA: What flavor?

GREEK BOY: Any flavor. It's what's inside that's special.

JOSH: What's inside?

GREEK GIRL: A coin.

SELENA: You put money inside the cake?

GREEK BOY: Yes.

JOSH: Why?

GREEK GIRL: The person who gets the slice of cake with the coin in it has extra good luck that year.

SELENA: That sounds like fun!

GREEK BOY: Here. Take this coin and make your own cake.

JOSH: [handing a noisemaker to the Greek boy and girl]

Thanks! Here are noisemakers that we use to celebrate the New Year.

GREEK BOY:	Thanks!
SELENA:	Happy New Year!
GREEK GIRL:	KALO PODARIKO to you, too!
	[pronounced KAH-low pah-DAH-rih-koh]
NARRATOR 1:	Josh and Selena climb back inside the Super Speedy Shuttle.
NARRATOR 2:	They and their Greek friends wave goodbye.
	[Greek boy and girl exit]
SELENA:	I think we have time for one more stop.
JOSH:	[looking at the map] Enter latitude 55.55 N, longitude 3.10 W.
	[pronounced fifty-five point fifty-five North; three point ten West]
	We're on our way to Edinburgh, Scotland.
	[pronounced ED-in-bruh; the "uh" is pronounced like the "a" in "above"]
SELENA:	Not until you press the "return" button.
NARRATOR 1:	Josh pushes the button. [Offstage machine noises]
	[Josh and Selena shake in their chairs]

Scene 8—Scotland

SETTING: Onstage are Narrator 1, Narrator 2, Josh, and Selena. Entering from stage left or right are a Scottish boy and girl. The location is Edinburgh, Scotland. [Josh and Selena stop shaking; sound of machine noises stops]

NARRATOR 1:	Josh and Selena climb out of the Super Speedy Shuttle.
NARRATOR 2:	They're in Edinburgh, the capital city of Scotland.
NARRATOR 1:	A Scottish boy and girl walk by.
SCOTTISH GIRL:	Happy Hogmanay! [pronounced HOG-man-aye]
JOSH:	Happy Hogmanay?
SCOTTISH BOY:	It's how we say Happy New Year.
SELENA:	Where are you going?
SCOTTISH GIRL:	We're going home to get ready for first footing.
JOSH:	What's first footing?

SCOTTISH BOY:	It's when the Dark Stranger comes to our house and is the first to put his foot in our house for the New Year.
SELENA:	Why does he do that?
SCOTTISH GIRL:	He brings good luck.
JOSH:	Who is the Dark Stranger?
SCOTTISH BOY:	We don't know. That's why he's called a stranger.
SCOTTISH GIRL:	But he leaves gifts for us.
SCOTTISH BOY:	A piece of coal to warm our homes.
SCOTTISH GIRL:	And a black bun.
JOSH:	What's a black bun?
SCOTTISH BOY:	It's a fruity cake.
SELENA:	Yum!
NARRATOR 2:	Josh and Selena hear singing.
	[Offstage singing or recorded music playing "Auld Lang Syne"]
JOSH:	I know that song.
SCOTTISH BOY:	It's an old Scottish song.
SCOTTISH GIRL:	It's called "Auld Lang Syne."
JOSH:	What does it mean?
SCOTTISH BOY:	It's about remembering old friends.
SCOTTISH GIRL:	[handing paper to Selena] Here are the words.
	[The song can be sung or read here by one of the narrators or characters, or all together]
SELENA:	Thanks. Now we can sing it, too.
JOSH:	If we ever get home.
SELENA:	[handing a noisemaker to the Scottish boy and girl]
	Here's one of our New Year noisemakers.
SCOTTISH BOY and GIRL:	Thanks.
SELENA:	Happy New Year!
SCOTTISH BOY and GIRL:	Happy Hogmanay! [Scottish boy and girl wave and exit]
NARRATOR 1:	Josh and Selena climb back into the Super Speedy Shuttle.
NARRATOR 2:	But they have a problem.
JOSH:	[reading instructions] How do we get back to our house?
SELENA:	Can we figure out the latitude and longitude from the map?
JOSH:	Our town isn't on this map.

SELENA: If we guess, we might end up miles away!

JOSH: [pointing] I've got an idea.

SELENA: [nodding] Let's try it.

NARRATOR 2: Josh pushes the "return" key.

[Offstage machine noises]

[Josh and Selena shake in their chairs]

[Josh and Selena stop shaking; sound of machine noises stops]

NARRATOR 1: It worked!

NARRATOR 2: The "return" key **returned** Josh and Selena home...

NARRATOR 1: Just in time to start their New Year celebration.

NARRATOR 2: They climb out of their Super Speedy Shuttle.

JOSH: Happy New Year!

SELENA: Wherever and whenever it is for YOU!

FOLLOW-UP ACTIVITIES

Where in the World Am I? (Geography)

On a world map, have students find the countries discussed in this chapter: The United States, China, South Korea, Venezuela, Australia, Greece, and Scotland. Locate the capital cities named in the play. Locate the major rivers, mountains, and cities in each country.

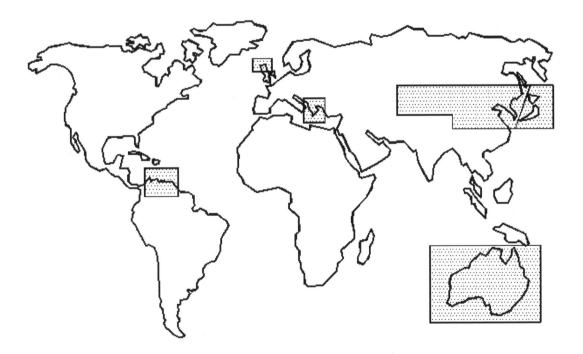

Make a Flag of Scotland (Math, Art)

Students make a flag from any of the countries represented in the play (USA, China, South Korea, Venezuela, Greece, Australia, or Scotland). These instructions are for students to make a flag of Scotland.

According to legend, during an eighth-century battle, a Scottish king asked God for help. A vision of Saint Andrew appeared and told the king he would win. The next day, a, white cross shape appeared sideways in the sky, and the Scots won the battle. The king knew that Saint Andrew had been killed for his faith by being hung to die on a sideways cross. To honor the miracle of Saint Andrew's sign in the sky, a white, sideways cross called a "saltire" [pronounced SOL-tir], against a sky-blue field, became the national flag of Scotland. To make a Scottish flag you will need:

❖ A sheet of white construction paper 9 inches by 12 inches

❖ Sheet of sky-blue paper 9 inches by 12 inches

❖ Ruler

❖ Pencil

❖ Scissors or paper cutter

❖ Glue

Using a ruler, pencil, and scissors, measure, mark, and cut the blue construction paper to 6 inches by 9 inches. Then measure, mark, and cut the white construction paper lengthwise into strips approximately 1¼ inch by 12 inches. NOTE: Paper can be precut using a paper cutter. Or to save paper, students can work in pairs—one student measuring and cutting the blue paper and one student measuring and cutting the white paper, to benefit from the math tie-in.

Place the blue sheet of paper in front of you horizontally. Glue strips of white paper onto the blue sheet to form an "X" centered on the blue paper. Cut the edges of the white strips even with the edges of the blue paper.

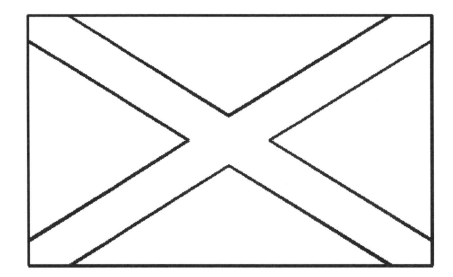

The Scottish flag ratio can be either 5:3 or 3:2 (length to width). The width of each bar of the saltier is one-fifth of the width of the flag. An additional class activity can include a discussion and calculation to make a different-sized flag, using either ratio.

National Anthem of Australia (Literacy, Music)

Read and discuss the lyrics of the national anthem of Australia. Check the library or online for a recording of the music.

> Australians all let us rejoice,
> For we are young and free,
> We've golden soil and wealth for toil;
> Our home is girt by sea;
> Our land abounds in nature's gifts
> Of beauty rich and rare;
> In history's page, let every stage
> Advance Australia Fair.
> In joyful strains then let us sing,
> Advance Australia Fair.
>
> Beneath our radiant Southern Cross
> We'll toil with hearts and hands
> To make this Commonwealth of ours
> Renowned of all the lands;
> For those who've come across the seas
> We've boundless plains to share,
> With courage let us all combine
> To Advance Australia Fair.
> In joyful strains then let us sing,
> Advance Australia Fair.

Discuss the words of Australia's National Anthem. Study the geography of Australia for hints to phrases in the anthem.

Find, read, and discuss national anthems of the other countries visited by Josh and Selena: China, South Korea, Venezuela, Greece, and Scotland. Write a cooperative or individual anthem for your town or school.

Currency Conversion (Math)

Using an online currency converter or the financial section of the newspaper, look up the types of money used in the countries Josh and Selena visited: China (yuan), South Korea (won), Venezuela (Bolivar), Greece (euro), Australia (Australian dollar), and Scotland (pound). How does each currency compare to a United States dollar? Calculate how much it would cost in each country's currency to buy:

❖ A candy bar (at US $.50)

❖ A pizza (at US $10.00)

❖ A car (at US $15,000.00)

HAVE A NEW YEAR CELEBRATION

Dress in costumes from the countries Josh and Selena visited. Check the library for background music from those countries.

Snack on grapes. Give each student 12 grapes. Have a clock that chimes or beeps the number of the hour. Set it for twelve o'clock or have one person bang a gong to simulate a clock chime. Students eat one grape for each chime (chew fast!).

Ahead of time, make a Greek "Vasilopita" New Year cake. Wrap a penny tightly in foil and stir it into the cake batter before baking. After the cake is baked, slice and serve the cake to see who gets the coin. Have everyone pick through their piece of cake and find the coin before eating, so no one accidentally swallows it. Have plates or napkins and a serving knife. The cake doesn't need to be frosted. The fun is seeing who gets the coin!

Seesaw (Science)

For this activity you will need:

- ❖ Several bricks

- ❖ A piece of wood approximately 6 inches wide and 2 to 3 feet long

- ❖ Several objects of similar and different weights—such as several books, pencil pouches, erasers, juice boxes

Introduce and discuss the concepts of fulcrum and balance. Stack the bricks in a pile to create a fulcrum. Center the wood over the stack. Experiment and discuss what happens if a heavy object is placed on one end of the wood and a light object is placed on the other. How does the distance from the center affect the seesaw? Experiment with weight and the position of objects on the board.

Chinese Paper Cutting (Math, Art)

Chinese paper cutting involves creating intricate pictures by cutting paper. The following simplified activity is similar to making paper snowflakes. You will need:

- ❖ Sheet of lightweight paper—any color

- ❖ Scissors

Fold the paper in half widthwise. Fold it again in half lengthwise; then again widthwise, and again lengthwise.

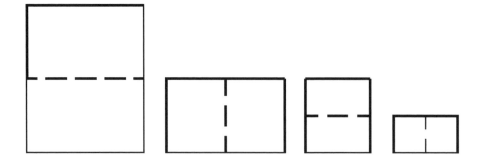

With scissors, snip into the folded edges of the paper, through all thicknesses. Use both straight and curved cuts, but keep the cuts small. Open the paper and spread it flat. Hang it in a window or glue it onto a sheet of paper in a contrasting color. Introduce and discuss the concept of **symmetry.**

Korean Yut Game (Math)

To play the Korean board game of Yut you will need:

- ❖ 4 dried beans

- ❖ Felt pen

- ❖ 4 buttons or place markers (mals) per player or team. Each set of 4 should be different from the other sets to avoid confusion.

- ❖ 1 Yut board

Traditionally, 4 Yut sticks are used—lengths of wood that are flat on one side and rounded on the other. The count is determined based on whether the side that's facing up is flat or rounded. For our game, we will use dried beans. Color one side of each bean with a felt pen.

The game starts with all mals (game pieces) at home. A player tosses the beans and moves a mal around the board the appropriate number of spaces, depending on the number of marked and unmarked sides of the beans that are up.

- ❖ **Do** 1 unmarked side up; 3 marked sides up—move 1 space

- ❖ **Gae** 2 unmarked sides up; 2 marked sides up—move 2 spaces

- ❖ **Gul** 3 unmarked sides up; 1 marked side up—move 3 spaces

- ❖ **Yut** 4 unmarked sides up—move 4 spaces

- ❖ **Mo** 4 marked sides up—move 5 spaces

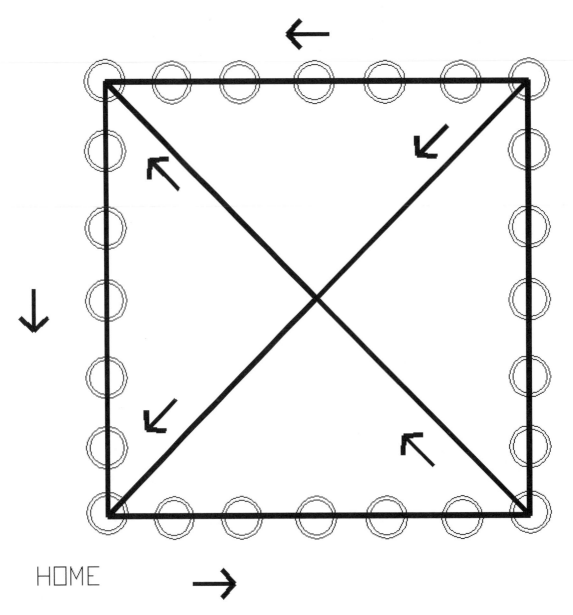

HOME

Move one mal each time the beans are thrown. If a mal lands on a corner, the player can take a diagonal shortcut through the middle of the board. Players who score Mo or Yut get a second turn. If two mals belonging to one player occupy the same space, they may then move together. If your mal lands on a space occupied by an opponent's mal, the opponent's mal is sent home and must begin again and you get another turn. The first player to get all of his or her mals around the board wins.

Discuss the geometry of a Yut board—square, triangle, angles, and circles.

Auld Lang Syne (Literacy, Music)

Read the lyrics of the song, "Auld Lang Syne." Research the life of the Scottish writer Robert Burns. Locate a recording of the song at the library or online and sing along.

Should auld acquaintance be forgot
and never brought to mind?
Should auld acquaintance be forgot
and days of auld lang syne?
For auld lang syne, my dear,
for auld lang syne,
we'll take a cup of kindness yet,
for auld lang syne.

Should auld acquaintance be forgot
and never brought to mind?
Should auld acquaintance be forgot
and days of auld lang syne?
And here's a hand, my trusty friend
And gie's a hand o' thine
We'll tak' a cup o' kindness yet
For auld lang syne

SUGGESTIONS FOR FURTHER ACTIVITIES

History: Research the evolution of our calendar from Roman times (Julian calendar, named after Julius Caesar) to our present calendar (Gregorian calendar, named after Pope Gregory, who adopted it). See the chapter entitled **Calendars.**

Social Studies: Research New Year customs and beliefs in more detail for any of the countries in this chapter, or for other countries of interest.

Geography/Literacy/Science/Math: Read through the script and note the latitudes and longitudes for the cities Josh and Selena visited. Use those latitudes and longitudes to locate the cities on a world map. Give the latitude and longitude but not the name of a city. The first person to call out the name of the city wins.

Language Arts: Have students write a poem or story about one of the country's New Year traditions or a tradition of their own.

Literacy: Josh and Selena learned New Year greetings in the countries they visited. Read through the script to find out the greetings in China, South Korea, Venezuela, Greece, and Scotland.

Science: Discuss a lunar month and how it relates to a month of our calendar. (See the chapter entitled **Calendars.**)

Science: Discuss the seasons of the year and why some cultures would consider spring to be the New Year (plants returning to life), or why others would consider autumn to be a natural time for the New Year (harvest brings abundance).

Science: Research boomerangs, the science of aerodynamics, and how boomerangs are thrown and caught.

Math: Review a cake recipe. Discuss measurement conversions and practice converting fractions and whole numbers and ounces and metric measurements, using the recipe as a guide. (See the chapter entitled **Measurements and Metric Conversions.**)

February—Fastelavn

(Denmark)

BACKGROUND

Fastelavn [pronounced fast-uh-LAV-en] is usually celebrated in February just before Lent (the 40 days before Easter.) People often give up certain foods during Lent (such as meat, cream, and sugar) as a way to honor God, but they feast right before Lent to use up those foods before they stop eating them. The Christian holiday of Easter is determined partly by the Jewish holiday of Passover (see the chapter entitled **Passover**) and the Jewish lunar calendar. Because a lunar calendar does not coincide with our solar calendar, Easter, Lent, and Fastelavn do not fall on the same day each year. (See the chapter entitled **Calendars.**)

READERS THEATRE SCRIPT—TILTING THE BARREL

Suggested Costumes and Props

- ❖ Part of the fun of Fastelavn is dressing up in costumes. Danish children wear whatever costume they want for the Fastelavn party, so use imagination for Scenes 3 and 4. Wear street clothes for Scene 1; bathrobes or pajamas for Scene 2.

- ❖ Suitcases (Scene 1)

- ❖ Pillows and blankets (Scene 2)

- ❖ Decorated branches (Scene 2)

- ❖ Small bags to carry (Scene 3)

- ❖ Baseball bat (Scene 4)

❖ Barrel—(class activity, to use in the performance.) If you intend to perform the play more than once, use an imaginary bat during the performance (Scene 4).

❖ 2 gold crowns (Scene 4)

Characters

The following is a list of characters. Nonspeaking roles can include neighbors and other children at the party.

- NARRATOR 1
- NARRATOR 2
- KRISTEN
- ERIK
- GRETTE

- MIKKEL
- MOTHER
- FATHER
- NEIGHBOR

Presentation Suggestions

This play includes 4 scenes. Narrator 1, Narrator 2, Kristen, Erik, Grette, and Mikkel will be onstage at all times. Consider decorating the back of the stage with a large Danish flag or smaller flags made as a separate activity by each student. The **SETTING** at the beginning of each scene is to assist the characters and is not intended to be read. Performance suggestions (gestures, movements, facial expressions) and pronunciation helps are included in brackets.

Tilting the Barrel

Scene 1—Grette and Mikkel's House

SETTING: Denmark, at the home of Grette and Mikkel. Their American cousins, Kristen and Erik, have come to visit. Grette and Mikkel are "inside" the living room; Kristen and Erik are "outside." Also onstage are Narrator 1 and Narrator 2.

NARRATOR 1:	Kristen and Erik have come to Denmark from America to visit their cousins, Grette and Mikkel.
NARRATOR 2:	It is the day before Fastelavn.
	[pronounced fast-uh-LAV-en]
GRETTE:	Kristen! Erik! Velkommen!
	[pronounced VEL-cum-en]
MIKKEL:	You're just in time!
KRISTEN:	Time for what?
GRETTE:	Time to help us get ready.
ERIK:	Get ready for what?
MIKKEL:	For Fastelavn, of course!
KRISTEN:	What's Fastelavn?
GRETTE:	It's a holiday. Don't you celebrate Fastelavn?
ERIK:	We've never heard of it.
MIKKEL:	You're going to love it!
GRETTE:	Let's help Mother bake the cakes.
KRISTEN:	Cakes?
ERIK:	I love Fastelavn already!

From *Around the World Through Holidays: Cross Curricular Readers Theatre* written and illustrated by Carol Peterson.
Westport, CT: Teacher Ideas Press/Libraries Unlimited. Copyright © 2006.

Scene 2—Fastelavn Morning

SETTING: Kristen and Erik are sleeping on one side of the stage in one "room." Erik and Grette's parents are sleeping on the other side of the stage in another "room." Grette and Mikkel enter Kristen and Erik's room. Also onstage are Narrator 1 and Narrator 2.

NARRATOR 1:	The next morning Grette and Mikkel wake up Kristen and Erik.
NARRATOR 2:	Grette and Mikkel are carrying birch tree branches.
NARRATOR 1:	The branches are decorated with ribbons and candies.
GRETTE:	Kristen! Erik! Wake up!
MIKKEL:	[handing Kristen and Erik the branches]
	Here are your Lenten branches—we decorated them for you.
KRISTEN:	Thanks. They're pretty.
ERIK:	Why are you giving us branches?
GRETTE:	We wake up our parents by waving them.
ERIK:	Let's go!
NARRATOR 1:	They tiptoe into Grette and Mikkel's parents' room.
	[Grette, Mikkel, Kristen, and Erik tiptoe across the stage]
NARRATOR 2:	They wave the branches and shout.
GRETTE, MIKKEL, KRISTEN, & ERIK:	Wake up! Wake up!
FATHER:	Good morning! Happy Fastelavn!
MOTHER:	Happy Fastelavn! Let's go eat our Fastelavn cakes!
NARRATOR 1:	Everyone runs to the kitchen.
NARRATOR 2:	To eat cakes filled with cream.
	[Grette, Mikkel, Kristen, Erik, Father, and Mother cross the stage and pretend to eat]
KRISTEN:	These are great!
ERIK:	May I please have another?
MOTHER:	You'd better not eat too many or you'll be too full for the party!
KRISTEN:	There's a party?
ERIK:	Let's get ready now!

Scene 3—In Costume

SETTING: Erik and Grette's living room and out into the neighborhood. Onstage are Narrator 1, Narrator 2, Grette, Erik, Kristen, and Mikkel.

NARRATOR 1:	The kids got ready for the day.
NARRATOR 2:	Part of the fun of Fastelavn is dressing up in costume.
GRETTE:	Kristen and Erik, your costumes are great!
KRISTEN:	Thanks, so are yours.
ERIK:	Do we go to the party now?
GRETTE:	Not yet. First we knock on our neighbors' doors...
MIKKEL:	...and they give us coins or candy!
KRISTEN:	That's what we do at Halloween.
ERIK:	Let's go!
	[Grette, Erik, Kristen, and Mikkel walk around the stage as if walking outside, each one carrying a bag for goodies]
ERIK:	This is a fun holiday!
KRISTEN:	But what is the holiday about?
GRETTE:	Wednesday is the first day of Lent.
ERIK:	What is Lent?
GRETTE:	Lent is the 40 days before Easter.
MIKKEL:	After Wednesday, no one gets to eat sweets.
KRISTEN:	For a whole 40 days?
GRETTE & MIKEL:	Yes! For a WHOLE 40 days!
ERIK:	I couldn't last 40 days without sweets.
GRETTE:	That's why we have such a big party today.
MIKKEL:	After stuffing yourself, you'll be ready to give up sweets later!
ERIK:	I'll never be ready to give up sweets.
KRISTEN:	Last Halloween you ate so much candy you felt sick.
ERIK:	Yeah, but 40 days is a long time!
KRISTEN:	Why do you give up sweets for Lent?
GRETTE:	Lent is a serious time in our religion.
MIKKEL:	People are supposed to remember that Jesus Christ died just before Easter.

ERIK:	But I thought Easter is a happy time.
GRETTE:	Easter IS happy. It's when Jesus came back from the dead.
MIKKEL:	It makes us even happier when Easter comes.
NARRATOR 1:	The children stop at a door.
ERIK:	So we just knock on the door and they give us money or candy?
MIKKEL:	When they answer the door, we're supposed to sing a song about Fastelavn cakes.
KRISTEN:	How does the song go?
GRETTE & MIKKEL:	[children may either sing or speak the following]
	Buns up, buns down, buns in my tummy. If I don't get any buns, I'll make trouble.
KRISTEN:	If I don't get buns, I'll make trouble?
ERIK:	That really sounds like Halloween!
NARRATOR 2:	The neighbor answers the door.
NEIGHBOR:	[Pretends to open the door]
ERIK:	Trick-or-treat!
	[Everyone laughs]
ERIK:	I mean "Happy Fastelavn!"

Scene 4—The Party

SETTING: At a friend's house. There is a real or imaginary bat, a barrel, and 2 gold crowns onstage. Narrator 1, Narrator 2, Kristen, Eric, Grette, Mikkel and other children are onstage.

NARRATOR 1:	Kristen, Erik, Grette, and Mikkel arrive at the party.
NARRATOR 2:	Everyone is in costume.
ERIK:	My bag is full of candy and coins!
KRISTEN:	Are we supposed to buy anything special with the money?
MIKKEL:	Yes—more candy!
ERIK:	Cool!
GRETTE:	Oh! We're a little late for the party.

MIKKEL: [pointing to the line of children]

They've already started tilting the barrel.

NARRATOR 1:   Grette, Mikkel, Kristen, and Erik get in line.

NARRATOR 2:   The first child in line swings a bat at a barrel.

NARRATOR 1:   There is a picture of a black cat on one side of the barrel.

[Each child in line takes a turn hitting the barrel and the four speakers move up the line as they speak]

KRISTEN: Tilting the barrel?

ERIK: It looks like they're trying to hit a piñata!

[Pause as next child in line swings at the barrel]

MIKKEL: What's a piñata?

KRISTEN: It's sort of a decorated box that you hit with a bat to break it open.

GRETTE: That's a lot like our barrel!

[Pause as next child in line swings]

MIKKEL: What's inside a piñata?

ERIK: Candy! What's inside the barrel?

MIKKEL: Candy!

ERIK and MIKKEL: Cool!

[Pause as next child in line swings.]

KRISTEN: Why is there a picture of a black cat on the barrel?

MIKKEL: Many years ago there used to be a black cat INSIDE the barrel.

[Pause as next child in line swings]

KRISTEN: A real black cat?

GRETTE: Yes. People thought black cats were a symbol of the devil.

MIKKEL: So they put a black cat inside and made it very mad by hitting the barrel.

GREETE: When the barrel broke, the cat fell out and ran away.

MIKKEL: Taking evil with it.

KRISTEN: Poor kitty!

MIKKEL: I like the idea of it being filled with candy!

ERIK: Me too!

NARRATOR 1:   The line has moved up, and now it's Grette's turn.

NARRATOR 2:   Grette swings and hits the barrel.

EVERYONE:	Yea! The barrel is almost broken.
MIKKEL:	My turn.
NARRATOR 1:	Mikkel swings the bat.
NARRATOR 2:	He hits the barrel, too.
EVERYONE:	Oh! One more hit and the candy will fall out!
NARRATOR 1:	Erik takes the bat, turns, and looks at Kristen.
ERIK:	Here, Kristen. You're better at baseball than I am.
KRISTEN:	Thanks, Erik. But you were in line before me.
ERIK:	Let's hit it together!
KRISTEN:	Okay!
NARRATOR 1:	Together Erik and Kristen swing and hit the barrel.
NARRATOR 2:	The candy falls to the floor and everyone rushes to grab it.
	[All characters pretend to pick up the fallen candy]
NARRATOR 1:	Grette and Mikkel place two golden paper crowns on Kristen and Erik's heads.
NARRATOR 2:	Everyone claps and cheers.
ERIK:	What are the crowns for?
GRETTE:	You broke open the barrel.
MIKKEL:	So you're Fastelavn king and queen.
KRISTEN:	Thanks! Happy Fastelavn everyone!
ERIK:	This is VERY cool!

FOLLOW-UP ACTIVITIES

Where in the World Am I? (Geography)

Find Denmark on a world map. Locate the latitude and longitude of Denmark. Locate the major cities, rivers, and oceans of Denmark. Locate Copenhagen, the capital city of Denmark, at latitude 55.40 N; longitude 12.34 E.

Make a Flag of Denmark (Math, Art)

The Danish flag is called a "Dannebrog," which means "Danish cloth." The design of the flag is a white cross set slightly to the left of center on a field of red. White on flags often represents peace. The cross is a symbol of the Christian religion. To make a Danish flag you will need:

- ❖ half sheet of red construction paper (cut to 4½ inches by 6 inches)
- ❖ half sheet of white 9-inch by 12-inch construction paper(cut to 4½ inches by 6 inches)
- ❖ Ruler
- ❖ Pencil
- ❖ Scissors
- ❖ Glue

Using the ruler and pencil, measure, mark, and cut 2 strips of white construction paper ¾ inches wide. Then measure, mark, and cut one of the strips to 4½ inches in length.

Place the half sheet of red paper in front of you horizontally. With the ruler and pencil, measure and mark a point 1 inch from the left edge of the red paper. Glue the 4½-inch strip of white paper at that mark vertically. With a ruler, measure and mark a point 2 inches from the top of the red paper and glue the 6-inch strip of white paper at that mark horizontally to create a white cross.

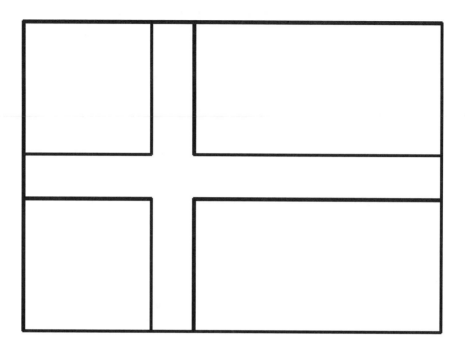

Use the flags to decorate the classroom or stage. NOTE: Making a Danish flag from half of a 9-inch by 12-inch piece of paper will be approximate. The actual ratio of the Danish flag is 28:37 (width to length). The dimensions of an official 28- by 37-inch flag from top to bottom would be: 12-inch red field followed by a 4-inch white field (horizontal bar of the cross) followed by a 12-inch red field. From left to right the dimensions would be: 12-inch red field followed by a 4-inch white field (vertical bar of the cross) followed by a 21-inch red field. Recalculate a different sized flag, using the same ratios, as an additional math activity.

National Anthem of Denmark (Literacy, Music, Geography, Social Studies)

Denmark has two official national anthems. Here are the words to the first verse of one of them. Check the library or look online for a recording of the music.

I know a lovely land
With spreading, shady beeches
Near Baltic's salty strand;
Its hills and valleys gently fall,
Its ancient name is Denmark,
And it is Freya's hall.

Discuss the lyrics as they relate to Denmark's geography and resources (Baltic Sea, Denmark's hills and valleys, and beech trees). Freya is a goddess from Norse mythology. Norse refers to the Scandinavian culture in the countries of Denmark, Norway, and Sweden. Look at a world map and discuss why the cultures and histories of those countries might be related.

Currency Conversion (Math)

The currency used in Denmark is the krone [pronounced KRO-nuh]. Check an online currency converter or the financial section of a newspaper and compare one krone with one US dollar. Calculate how much different items would cost in krones compared to dollars.

❖ A candy bar (at US $.50)

❖ A pizza (at US $10.00)

❖ A car (at US $15,000.00)

HAVE A FASTELAVN CELEBRATION

Dress in costume and enjoy Danish pastries. Ladyfingers are available at most grocery stores, or students might like to make them at home. If the class has access to an oven, they can be made as a class project. Then play Tilt the Barrel, make crowns, and declare everyone Fastelavn king and queen.

Ladyfingers Recipe (Math)

Danish pastries are light cakes often filled with heavy egg custard or cream. Ladyfingers are a Danish pastry shaped like fingers. Here is a simplified recipe. To make one dozen cakes you will need:

❖ 1 cup sugar

❖ 5 eggs

❖ ¼ teaspoon salt

❖ 1 cup flour

❖ 1 teaspoon vanilla

❖ Powdered sugar

❖ Sifter

❖ Cookie press or pastry bag

❖ Cookie sheet

❖ Bowl

❖ Electric mixer

❖ Oven mitt

❖ Metal spatula

❖ Custard or whipped cream (optional)

Wash hands before cooking. Preheat oven to 350 degrees. Beat sugar, eggs, vanilla, and salt together until frothy. Sprinkle flour over the egg mixture and mix lightly. Fill a cookie press or large pastry bag with batter and squeeze out finger-shaped cakes onto an ungreased cookie sheet. Bake for 7 minutes or until light brown. Cool on the cookie sheet and then sprinkle with powdered sugar from the sifter. Ladyfingers can be split open and filled with custard or whipped cream.

Tilting the Barrel Activity (Art, Physical Education)

Make a barrel, then fill it with candy and black paper cats. Break it open at an outdoor class Fastelavn party. To make a barrel you will need:

❖ A medium-weight box—heavy enough to withstand a few good whacks with a bat, but not so sturdy that it will not break open.

❖ Small pieces of candy or toys

❖ Wrapping paper

❖ Masking tape

❖ Picture of black cat for the front

❖ Paper black cats made as a class activity (optional)

❖ Markers; other decorations

❖ Rope or twine—enough to tie around the box and hang it from a tree limb or basketball hoop

❖ Tree limb or basketball hoop for hanging

❖ Baseball bat

Fill the box with candy, toys, and paper cats. Tape the box shut and cover it with wrapping paper. Glue a picture of a black cat on the front of the box. Tie the box with twine and hang it from a tree limb or basketball hoop.

Students may take turns swinging at the "barrel" with a baseball bat. When the box breaks open, all students share the treats. For a simpler alternate activity, decorate and fill a paper grocery bag instead of a box.

Discuss the cultural similarities and differences between the Fastelavn barrel and a Mexican piñata. (See the chapter entitled **Las Posadas.**)

Lenten Branches (Art, Science)

Part of the fun of Fastelavn is making Lenten branches. Cut short branches from any tree or bush. Strip away its leaves so that the branches are bare. Cut ribbons of various colors into lengths of 8 to 10 inches and tie them to the branch. The Lenten branches can be used in the play or to decorate the classroom.

Calculate the Height of a Tree (Math)

Birch trees are traditionally used as Lenten branches because they are one of the first trees to bud in spring. Discuss how the renewal of nature would especially encourage people in northern countries to celebrate springtime. Introduce, compare, and contrast evergreen and deciduous trees.

Try calculating the height of a tree, your school building, a flagpole, or playground equipment. You will need:

❖ Ruled triangle

❖ Long tape measure

❖ Paper

❖ Pencil

❖ Something to mark the ground (chalk for blacktop or cement; a rock for a grassy area)

❖ Calculator

Hold a ruled triangle at eye level with the right angle away from your face. Walk forward or backward until the top of the triangle is even with the top of the tree. Stop and mark the ground at your toes.

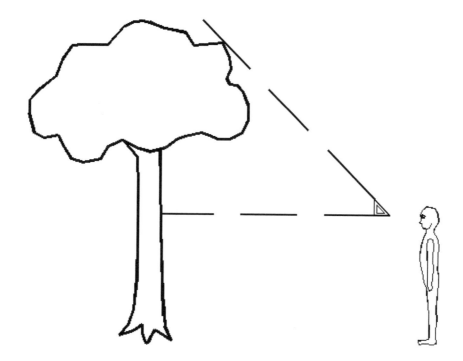

With a tape measure, measure the ground from your mark to the tree. With a calculator, convert that figure into inches by multiplying the number of feet times 12 and adding any leftover inches. Then have someone measure you from your feet to your eyes. Convert that figure into inches by multiplying the number of feet times 12 and adding any leftover inches. Add your height to the ground measurement. That equals the height of the tree in inches. Divide that figure by 12 to get the height of the tree in feet plus remaining inches.

Why does this work? The triangle is an isosceles right triangle, which means both sides of the right angle are the same length. Therefore, when you line it up with the tree, the distance from your feet to the tree plus your height is the same as the height of the tree.

Danish Folk Dance (Physical Education)

Locate recordings of Danish music from the library and learn a Danish folk dance. One folk dance is called the "2-Trip from Vejile." For this dance, stand boy-girl-boy-girl in a circle, facing toward the center. Everyone joins hands and circles to the right for 8 counts.

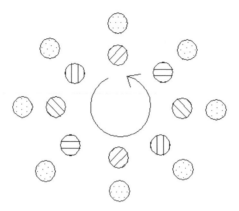

Then circle to the left for 8 counts.

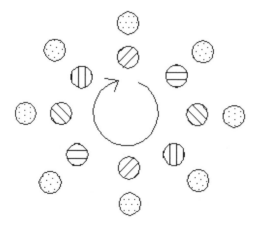

Drop hands and pair off into couples. Each couple joins hands (boy's right hand; girl's left hand), turns toward the center of the circle, and walks toward the center (boy on the left; girl on the right). Sing "One and two and we say 'hi.'" On "hi," raise the two joined hands.

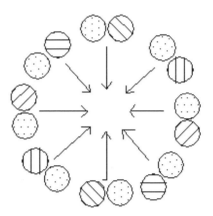

Turn right and walk away from the center.

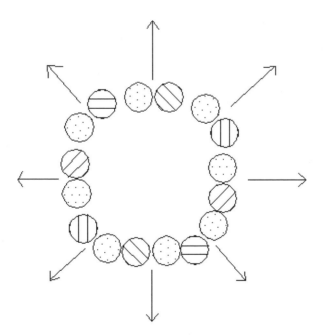

Each couple then walks in a circle right while the entire group is circling to the left.

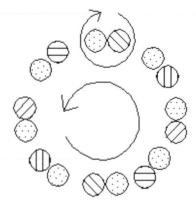

Repeat.

Golden Crowns (Art, Math)

To make Fastelavn crowns you will need:

❖ One sheet of yellow construction paper, 18 inches by 24 inches (will make two crowns per illustration)

❖ Scissors

❖ Stapler

❖ Colored marking pens, gold glitter, glue and other decorations, as desired

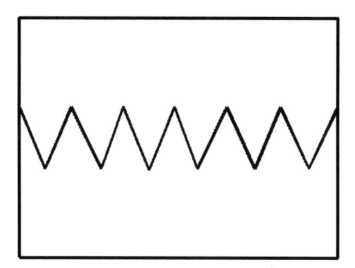

The paper crowns used at Fastelavn are traditionally gold, so students may want to decorate their crowns with glitter. When decorated, wrap each crown around the student's head to mark its size, then remove it and staple the ends. Wear during the Fastelavn celebration.

Using a protractor, measure the angles of the points of the crown. Discuss what happens to the angles if more or fewer points are used within the same length of paper.

Black Cats (History, Science, Art)

Long ago, a live cat was placed inside the Fastelavn barrel to represent the devil. Fortunately for cats, today a picture or toy cat is used. In this activity, students draw black cats to be placed in the barrel along with the candy, or as classroom or stage decorations. To make a black cat you will need:

- ❖ One sheet of black 9-inch by 12-inch construction paper—cut in half to 9 inches by 6 inches

- ❖ Pencil

- ❖ Scissors

- ❖ Markers

Draw a black cat on the construction paper and cut it out. Discuss superstitions about black cats and how cats were thought to represent evil. Use the following points to start a discussion:

- ❖ Superstition led to people killing cats

- ❖ Killing cats meant more rodents

- ❖ Rodents carried fleas

- ❖ Fleas carried the black plague throughout Europe

- ❖ 25 million people (one-third the population of Europe) died from the plague in five years

SUGGESTIONS FOR FURTHER ACTIVITIES

History: Compare and contrast Fastelavn with Halloween—costumes, going door to door, parties, superstitions about black cats. Research other countries' Lenten festivals—Carnivale in South America, Mardi Gras in New Orleans, Pancake Day in England, Blini Day in Russia. Note that Mardi Gras in French means "fat Tuesday." Discuss **fat** in terms of the rich, cream-filled Fastelavn buns and everyone's bellies the day after!

Social Studies: Research Denmark—its form of government today (constitutional monarchy), traditional folk costumes, music.

Literacy/Language Arts: Learn some Danish words:

English	**Danish**
Thank you very much	Mange tak
Good-bye	Farvel
Yes	Ja
No	Nej

Literacy: Read a version of the *The Little Mermaid*, by Hans Christian Andersen. Research her statue in the harbor of Copenhagen. Who was the sculptor? What is the statue made of? Where is she looking? What might she be thinking?

Science: Discuss a lunar month and how it relates to a month of our calendar. (See the chapter entitled **Calendars.**)

Science: Discuss the northern latitudes' location on the earth in relation to the sun and how that affects weather and unusual topography, such as icebergs and fjords.

Science/Geography: Greenland is officially part of the Kingdom of Denmark. Northern lights are seen frequently in Greenland and occasionally in Denmark. Research the northern lights. Discuss what life would be like with only a few hours of darkness in the summer and a few hours of daylight in the winter. Compare the latitudes of other places where the northern lights can be seen.

Literacy/Language Arts: There are many myths associated with the northern lights. One Danish myth explains that the lights are swans frozen in the ice. Read other myths about the northern lights from the countries where the lights can be seen. Have students write their own myth to explain the lights.

March—Happy St. Patrick's Day

(Ireland)

BACKGROUND

This holiday celebrates the life of a Roman Catholic priest. St. Patrick was not born in Ireland. He was born into a wealthy family around the year AD 385, probably in nearby Wales. He was kidnapped and taken to Ireland as a slave. After he escaped, he became a Roman Catholic priest and then returned to Ireland to convert his former captors to Christianity.

READERS THEATRE SCRIPT—KIDNAPPED!

Suggested Costumes and Props

- ❖ Paper chains (Scenes 1 and 2)
- ❖ Chairs to represent a boat (Scenes 2, 3, and 4)
- ❖ Pole for shepherd's staff (Scene 2)
- ❖ Large shamrock for Patrick (Scene 6)
- ❖ Robe for Patrick (Scenes 5 and 6)
- ❖ White robe for the Pope (Scene 5)
- ❖ Robes for Priest 1, Priest 2, and Priest 3 (Scene 6)
- ❖ Shawls or aprons for women; hats for men (Scene 6)
- ❖ Paper snakes (Scene 6)

Characters

The following is a list of characters. Different students may play the roles of Young Maewyn, Older Maewyn, and Patrick.

- NARRATOR 1
- NARRATOR 2
- YOUNG MAEWYN
- OLDER MAEWYN
- PATRICK
- SERVANT 1
- SERVANT 2
- SLAVE 1
- SLAVE 2
- KIDNAPPERS
- CHIEF MILIUC

- SHIP CAPTAIN
- SAILOR 1
- SAILOR 2
- SAILOR 3
- POPE
- PRIEST 1
- PRIEST 2
- PRIEST 3
- VILLAGER 1
- VILLAGER 2
- VILLAGER 3

Presentation Suggestions

This play includes 6 scenes. Narrator 1 and Narrator 2 will be onstage at all times. Consider decorating the back of the stage area with a landscape drawn on butcher paper, a large flag of Ireland, smaller flags made by students, or shamrocks. The **SETTING** at the beginning of each scene is to assist the characters and is not intended to be read. Performance suggestions (gestures, movements, facial expressions) and pronunciation helps are included in brackets.

Kidnapped!

Scene 1—The Kidnapping

SETTING: The time is the late AD 300s in Wales. Onstage are Narrator 1, Narrator 2, Young Maewyn, Servant 1, Servant 2, and one kidnapper or more.

NARRATOR 1: The time is the end of the fourth century in the land we call Wales.

NARRATOR 2: Wales is now part of Great Britain.

NARRATOR 1: But in the fourth century, England, Wales, and Ireland were part of the Roman Empire.

NARRATOR 2: Young Maewyn was 16 years old.

[pronounced MAY-win]

NARRATOR 1: His wealthy father worked for the Roman government.

NARRATOR 2: At that time, Ireland was called Hibernia.

[pronounced high-BER-nee-ah]

NARRATOR 1: Tribes from Hibernia would sometimes come to Wales.

NARRATOR 2: They would kidnap people and take them as slaves.

NARRATOR 1: One day they came to Maewyn's village.

SERVANT 1: Maewyn, run for it!

SERVANT 2: Young master, hide!

KIDNAPPERS: Get them!

SERVANT 1: No!

SERVANT 2: Let us go!

MAEWYN: Help!

NARRATOR 1: The kidnappers caught Maewyn and his servants.

[Kidnappers tie Maewyn and his servants with chains]

NARRATOR 2: They took them to Hibernia.

From *Around the World Through Holidays: Cross Curricular Readers Theatre* written and illustrated by Carol Peterson. Westport, CT: Teacher Ideas Press/Libraries Unlimited. Copyright © 2006.

Scene 2—To Hibernia

SETTING: The journey by boat to Hibernia. Onstage in the "boat" are Maewyn, his servants, the kidnappers, other nonspeaking kidnapped slaves (optional). Later, Chief Miliuc enters from stage left or stage right. Characters may sit on chairs or the floor to represent the boat.

NARRATOR 1:   Maewyn and his servants were put on board the ship.

NARRATOR 2:   It took them to Hibernia.

[Maewyn, servants, and kidnappers pretending to row]

NARRATOR 1:   When they landed, they were taken to the Hibernia Chief Miliuc.

[Chief Miliuc and several of his people enter from stage left or stage right. Maewyn, his servants, and kidnappers get out of the boat]

CHIEF MILIUC: [pointing to Maewyn] You, there, boy! And you two! Go to the field and take care of my sheep! I've got other plans for the rest of you.

[The others exit, leaving Narrator 1, Narrator 2, Maewyn, and two servants on stage]

MAEWYN: God must be punishing me!

NARRATOR 1:   Maewyn was a slave for many years.

NARRATOR 2:   He often thought about escaping and returning home.

MAEWYN: If only we could escape!

SLAVE 1:   It's too dangerous. Runaway slaves are killed!

SLAVE 2:   And how would we get home?

SLAVE 1:   It's miles and miles to the ocean.

SLAVE 2:   We have no boat even if we could get to the ocean.

MAEWYN: You're right. We'd never make it.

NARRATOR 1:   Maewyn decided to trust God.

NARRATOR 2:   Finally, after six years of slavery, Maewyn knew God wanted him to escape.

MAEWYN: I've got to escape.

SLAVE 1:   Don't go!

SLAVE 2:   You'll be caught!

MAEWYN: God wants me to try.

Scene 3—Back on a Ship

SETTING: At the ocean in Hibernia. Onstage are Narrator 1, Narrator 2, older Maewyn, a Captain, Sailor 1, Sailor 2, and Sailor 3.

NARRATOR 1:	Maewyn made his way over 200 miles to the ocean.
NARRATOR 2:	When he arrived, a ship was there.
OLDER MAEWYN:	[to the Captain] Please, Captain, may I travel with you to my home?
CAPTAIN:	Are you a runaway slave?
OLDER MAEWYN:	Yes, I was taken from my home when I was a boy.
CAPTAIN:	If I'm caught helping a runaway slave, I'm a dead man. Sorry, but I can't help you.
	[Captain exits]
NARRATOR 1:	So Maewyn prayed to ask what he should do.
NARRATOR 2:	Suddenly the captain changed his mind.
SAILOR 1:	Hey, kid!
SAILOR 2:	Come aboard.
SAILOR 3:	The captain changed his mind.

Scene 4—Shipwrecked

SETTING: Somewhere between Hibernia and home. Onstage are Narrator 1, Narrator 2, Older Maewyn, the Captain, Sailor 1, Sailor 2, and Sailor 3.

NARRATOR 1:	Maewyn boarded the ship.
NARRATOR 2:	But on the way a storm came up.
SAILOR 1:	The sea is rough today!
SAILOR 2:	I've never seen such a storm!
SAILOR 3:	The wind is so strong!
CAPTAIN:	Hold it steady, men!
	[Everyone moans and leans back and forth as if on a rocking boat]

NARRATOR 1:	The storm got worse.
NARRATOR 2:	Finally, the ship crashed.
	[Everyone except Narrator 1 and Narrator 2 pretends to swim toward either stage left or stage right. Then they stand together]
CAPTAIN:	Well, there goes our boat.
SAILOR 1:	What shall we do, Captain?
SAILOR 2:	Where are we?
SAILOR 3:	How will we survive?
CAPTAIN:	I don't know, men. We'll just do the best we can.
NARRATOR 1:	Maewyn and the sailors were stranded without food for a month.
NARRATOR 2:	Then Maewyn asked God for help.
MAEWYN:	[pointing] Look! Wild pigs!
	[The sailors run around on stage pretending to chase pigs]
SAILOR 1:	Catch that fat one! Quick!
SAILOR 2:	Got him!
SAILOR 3:	We'll have a feast tonight!
NARRATOR 1:	After that, Maewyn made it home.
NARRATOR 2:	He believed God was watching over him.

Scene 5—Maewyn's New Life

SETTING: Vatican City, Italy. Onstage are Narrator 1, Narrator 2, Patrick, and the Pope.

NARRATOR 1:	After Maewyn was safe he went to France.
NARRATOR 2:	There he studied religion and became a priest.
NARRATOR 1:	The Pope, who was head of the church, gave Maewyn a new name.
NARRATOR 2:	Maewyn's new name was Patrick.
NARRATOR 1:	Patrick spoke with the Pope.
PATRICK:	I want to go to Hibernia.
POPE:	Why would you want to return there?

PATRICK: The people there need to hear about God.

POPE: I'd think you would want to stay far away from there after living there as a slave.

PATRICK: That's why I need to go back there. They need to hear what I have to say.

POPE: Then take some other priests with you.

PATRICK: Thank you.

Scene 6—Back in Hibernia

SETTING: Hibernia. Onstage are Narrator 1, Narrator 2, Patrick, Priest 1, Priest 2, Priest 3, Villager 1, Villager 2, and Villager 3.

NARRATOR 1: Patrick and his priests went to Hibernia.

NARRATOR 2: At first the Irish people didn't want to hear what Patrick had to say.

PRIEST 1: Patrick, these people want to do magic.

PRIEST 2: And they have secret ceremonies.

PRIEST 3: The chiefs are always trying to arrest us.

PATRICK: We just have to keep trying. And we have to explain things in a way they'll understand.

NARRATOR 1: So Patrick preached to the people.

NARRATOR 2: Over the next 30 years, Patrick and the priests traveled all over Ireland.

NARRATOR 1: They built many churches and schools.

NARRATOR 2: And Patrick spoke to the people in ways they would understand.

[Villagers gather around Patrick]

PATRICK: [holding a shamrock] Who can tell me what this plant is?

VILLAGER 1: It's a shamrock.

VILLAGER 2: Shamrocks grow everywhere.

PATRICK: Is each of the three leaves on a shamrock a separate plant?

VILLAGER 1: No, of course not.

VILLAGER 3: All three leaves are part of one shamrock.

PATRICK:	That's the same way it is with God.
VILLAGER 1:	What do you mean?
PATRICK:	The Father, the Son, and the Holy Spirit are three parts of the same being.
NARRATOR 1:	So Patrick explained his beliefs to the people of Hibernia.
NARRATOR 2:	He used things from their lives so they would understand what he was teaching.
NARRATOR 1:	There are many legends about St. Patrick. One legend says that he rid Ireland of snakes.
NARRATOR 2:	But there were no snakes in Ireland before Patrick was there.
NARRATOR 1:	The snakes were a symbol of people who didn't believe in God.
NARRATOR 2:	After Patrick preached, the unbelievers (the snakes) were gone.
	[Everyone except Narrator 1 and Narrator 2 waves paper snakes and exits]
NARRATOR 1:	St. Patrick died on March 17, AD 461.
NARRATOR 2:	The church gave him the title of "Saint," to recognize the work he did for God.
NARRATOR 1:	Now the world remembers St. Patrick on the date of his death. . .
NARRATOR 2:	. . .to celebrate his life.

FOLLOW-UP ACTIVITIES

Where in the World Am I? (Geography)

Find the Republic of Ireland on a world map. Locate the capital city—Dublin—on a map of Ireland, using its latitude (53.20 N) and longitude (6.15 W). Locate the major rivers, mountains, and cities in Ireland. Find the latitudinal and longitudinal boundaries of Ireland.

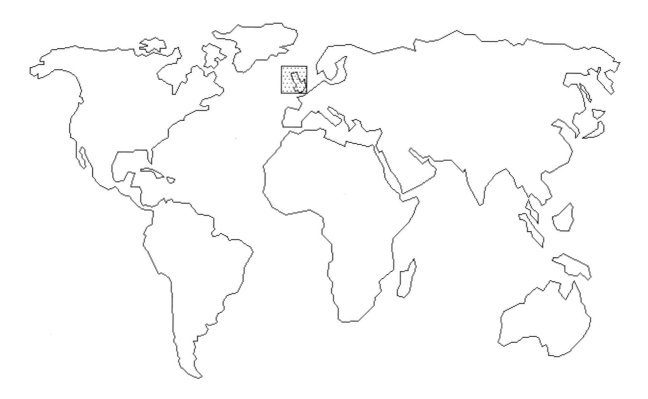

Make a Flag of Ireland (Math, Art)

The flag of the Republic of Ireland is called a "tricolor" because of its three colors. The green color represents the Catholic religion. The orange color represents the Protestant religion. The white between them represents peace between the two religions. Discuss modern day political fighting between Catholics and Protestants in Ireland. To make a flag of Ireland, you will need:

❖ 1 sheet of 9 inch by 12 inch white construction paper

❖ 1 sheet of 9 inch by 12 inch orange construction paper

❖ 1 sheet of 9 inch by 12 inch green construction paper

❖ Ruler

❖ Pencil

❖ Scissors or paper cutter

❖ Glue

The official ratio of the flag of Ireland is 1:2 (width to length). Using ruler, pencil, and scissors, measure, mark, and cut the white paper to a size 6 inches by 12 inches. Then measure, mark, and cut the green and orange paper to a size 6 inches by 4 inches. NOTE: Paper can be cut ahead of time with a paper cutter, or students can work together and share papers, thus benefiting from the math tie-in. Place the white paper in front of you horizontally. Glue the green paper onto the white sheet at the left side, matching edges. Glue the orange paper onto the white sheet at the right side, matching edges.

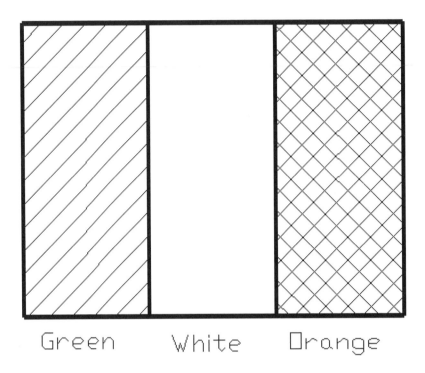

Green   White   Orange

Introduce the prefix "tri." Make a list of all the words in which the prefix "tri" means "three," and discuss the meaning of each word. Include the following and have students use a dictionary for more: triangle, tricycle, triple, trident, triathlon, triceratops, trilogy, trimester, trinity, triplet, triplex, triplicate, tripod). Do the same with the prefix "bi."

National Anthem of Ireland (Literacy, Music)

The national anthem of Ireland is called "A Soldier's Song." It was written in 1907 by Paedar Kearney. Here is the first verse and the chorus of that song. Check the library or look online for a recording of the music.

> We'll sing a song, a soldier's song,
> With cheering rousing chorus,
> As round our blazing fires we throng,
> The starry heavens o'er us;
> Impatient for the coming fight,
> And as we wait the morning's light,
> Here in the silence of the night,
> We'll chant a soldier's song.

Soldiers are we
Whose lives are pledged to Ireland;
Some have come
From a land beyond the wave.
Sworn to be free,
No more our ancient sire land
Shall shelter the despot or the slave.
Tonight we man the gap of danger
In Erin's cause, come woe or weal
'Mid cannons' roar and rifles peal,
We'll chant a soldier's song.

Currency Conversion (Math)

Two forms of currency are used on the island of Ireland. The Irish punt is used in the Republic of Ireland. The British pound sterling is used in Northern Ireland, which remained a part of the United Kingdom when the Republic of Ireland was granted independence. Check an online currency converter or the financial section of a newspaper and compare one punt and one pound with one US dollar. Also compare a punt with a pound. Calculate how much it would cost in each country's currency to buy:

❖ A candy bar (at US $.50)

❖ A pizza (at US $10.00)

❖ A car (at US $15,000.00)

HAVE A ST. PATRICK'S DAY CELEBRATION

Snack on potato chips, sausage, ham, potatoes, scones, or trifle and tea.

Trifle (Math)

A trifle is a dessert made with cake, jam, pudding, and fruit. It is layered in a deep, clear bowl. It is usually made a day or two ahead of time so that all the flavors mix together and the cake is extra soft from the moist pudding. To make trifle for 10 to 12 students you will need:

❖ Large bowl—transparent, if possible, so you can see the layering

❖ Pre-made custard or vanilla pudding (approximately 3 cups)

❖ Serving spoon

❖ Cake (pound or angel food)

❖ Small jar of raspberry jam

❖ Spreading knife

❖ Sharp knife for cutting cake

❖ Paper plates

❖ Spoons

Wash hands before cooking. Cut cake into 1-inch slices. Spread jam on the cake. Arrange one third of the cake slices in the bottom of a deep bowl. Spread a layer of custard or pudding on top of the cake. Arrange a second layer of cake and spread with a second layer of custard. Repeat with a third layer of each ending with a final layer of custard. Cover and refrigerate several hours, or overnight.

Paper Chains (Math, Art)

Make paper chains as props for the play. Use a ruler to measure specific lengths and widths of strips. Calculate how many strips can be made from a single sheet of construction paper if strips are 1 inch wide. Calculate how many strips can be made if they are 1½ inches wide. How many if they are 2 inches wide?

Use different colors of paper and discuss patterning. Have each student create a color pattern and explain it to the class. For example, a repeating pattern of a chain made from red, blue, red, and green paper would have a pattern of ABAC ABAC.

Shamrocks (Science, Art)

Make shamrocks using 3 heart patterns and a stem. Fold a sheet of green paper in half. With the fold on the right hand edge, use a pencil to draw a "C." Then cut out and open. Using that first heart as a pattern, trace and cut out a second and third heart. Glue the three hearts onto a sheet of paper. Cut out a stem from the scraps of green paper and glue it to the bottom of the shamrock.

Research shamrocks. Locate where they grow in the world, what they look like, what type of climate they need. What makes Ireland an ideal location for them to grow?

Leprechaun Footprints (Language Arts, Art)

Make leprechaun trails with water-based green paint. Make a fist with your thumb pointing up and dip the bottom of your fist into green paint. Press onto a surface. This forms the leprechaun's foot.

Then dip one finger into the green paint and make "toe" prints. Use both hands to create left and right footprints. Have soap and water handy for cleanup.

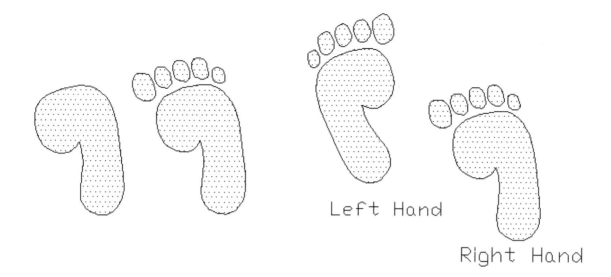

Left Hand

Right Hand

Paint footprints on paper to decorate the classroom or stage—or paint them around the schoolyard. Make a game for lower grade classes and have children follow the footprints on the playground to find a note or prize. Write a story to tell who made the footprints and what the leprechauns were up to.

Celtic Designs (Math, Art)

Celtic [pronounced KEL-tik] designs involve lines that connect and intertwine. They are reminders of fancy knots tied for decoration. To make these designs you will need:

❖ Paper

❖ Pencil

❖ Ruler

❖ Compass

❖ Marking pens

Using the Celtic patterns provided or those from other sources, design a St. Patrick's Day greeting card. Or create a Celtic design to make an "illuminated manuscript" for limericks.

Discuss the use of a compass for drawing circles and arcs. Introduce the concept of **symmetry.**

Limericks (Language Arts, Literacy, Geography, History, Math)

A limerick is a form of poetry that follows a special pattern. The limerick's AABBA pattern means that the first, second, and fifth lines each have 8 syllables and rhyme with each other. The middle 2 lines (third and fourth lines) each have 6 syllables and rhyme with each other separately from the first, second, and fifth lines. Have students write limericks using the following writing prompts, or one of their own. A limerick is meant to be funny, so the rhymes can be silly.

Give students a writing prompt for a limerick. The following words may help with rhyming inspiration.

First line: "We celebrate St. Patrick's Day"
  Rhyming hints for lines two and five:

way	say	may	hey	hay	tray
gray	play	lay	pay	pray	bay
gay	jay	stay	stray	spray	sleigh
weigh	they	okay	Bombay		

First line: "St. Patrick's real name was Maewyn"
  Rhyming hints for lines two and five:

in	inn	skin	chin	fin	shin
thin	twin	grin	sin	tin	bin
pin	win				

First line: "In Ireland it's grassy and green"
  Rhyming hints for lines two and five:

bean	keen	lean	mean	preen	seen
teen	clean	queen	screen	scene	sheen
praline	caffeine	between	Halloween		

The limerick became popular in the 1700s when Irish soldiers sang them on their way home from battle. Limerick is a town in Ireland. Locate it on a map of Ireland.

Discuss how math and language arts are both important parts of poetry. Research and discuss other types of poetry and the set rhythms used in each type. Compare the concepts of a poetic, rhyming pattern with the patterning discussed in the paper chain activity.

Brainstorming Saints (Literacy)

After his death on March 17, AD 461, the Roman Catholic Church granted Patrick the status of "Saint." A "Saint" (with a capital "S") is a special title granted to Christians whose lives were particularly important to the church. Since a person can't be given the title of a Saint until he dies, St. Patrick's Day is celebrated on the date of Patrick's death.

On what other holidays do people recognize Saints? (St. Valentine, St. Nicholas) Discuss other titles given to people—for example, Doctor (Dr.), Mister (Mr.), Missus. Make a list of all the titles and their abbreviations you can think of.

SUGGESTIONS FOR FURTHER ACTIVITIES

History: Research the history of the Roman Empire in Ireland.

History/Geography/Language Arts: The Blarney Stone is located at Blarney Castle, near the city of Cork in Southern Ireland. Read a version of the legend of how kissing the stone will give the kisser the power of eloquent speech (or lies) for 7 years. Introduce the literary technique of hyperbole, and have students write a "tall tale."

Literacy: Find and read Irish folktales. Research common legends and symbols of St. Patrick's Day (shamrocks, leprechauns, pot of gold, snakes) and where they came from.

Literacy: Celtic is a family of languages that includes Irish, Scottish Gaelic, Welsh, Cornish, Manx Gaelic, and Breton. Discuss how people's languages relate to the region where they live.

Science: Research snakes—how they move; what they eat; their skeletal system.

Science: Potatoes are a major food in Ireland Cut a potato in half, poke toothpicks around the center of it and place it in a jar of water, cut end up, so that a portion of the skin-covered end is immersed in water. Over the next few days or weeks observe the potato as the "eyes" sprout.

History/Literacy: Make a list of all the ways you can cook and eat potatoes. Discuss how the potato harvest from 1846 to 1850 in Ireland led to famine and disease from eating rotten potatoes. Discuss why so many people emigrated from Ireland to the United States during the famine. Introduce the terms "emigrate" and "immigrate."

Math/Art: Make long strips of paper 1 to 2 inches wide. Decorate them as snakes. Wind them around your finger to curl and use them as props in Scene 3.

Math: When making the trifle, include a discussion of fractions and whole numbers, and standard and metric system conversions. (See the chapter entitled **Measurements and Metric Conversions**.)

April—Passover

(Israel)

BACKGROUND

Passover is an 8-day Jewish holiday to celebrate God's deliverance of the people from slavery in Egypt, in about the year 1250 BC. It is generally celebrated in March or April, based on the Jewish lunar calendar.

READERS THEATRE SCRIPT—ESCAPE TO FREEDOM

Suggested Costumes and Props

❖ Robes and shawls (Scenes 2, 4, 5, 7, 8)

❖ Basket (Scene 2)

❖ Staffs—such as broom handles—for Moses and Aaron (Scenes 2, 4, 5, 7, 8)

❖ Chair for Pharaoh's throne (Scenes 4, 5)

❖ Snake—rubber or paper (Scene 4)

❖ Slips of black paper for gnats, flies, and locusts—not too small for easy cleanup (Scene 5)

❖ White paper hail (Scene 5)

❖ Origami frogs or crumpled green paper (Scene 4)

❖ Paper or plastic Seder plate (Scenes 1, 3, 6, 9)

❖ Clear plastic glass filled with red paper (Scene 4)

❖ Red fabric or red construction paper to represent the Red Sea (Scene 8)

❖ Bundles of cloth and baskets for the exodus (Scene 8)

❖ Spears and shields for Pharaoh's army—yardsticks and decorated cardboard (Scene 8)

Characters

The following is a list of characters. One role is the PLAGUE BRINGER, who enacts the plagues sent to Egypt. Narrator 1 and Narrator 2 are onstage in Scenes 1, 3, 6, and 9 at the Rosen house. Narrator 3 and Narrator 4 are onstage in Scenes 2, 4, 5, 7, and 8 in ancient Egypt.

- NARRATOR 1 (modern time)
- NARRATOR 2 (modern time)
- NARRATOR 3 (ancient Egypt)
- NARRATOR 4 (ancient Egypt)
- DAVID
- SARAH
- FATHER ROSEN
- MOTHER ROSEN
- PHARAOH'S DAUGHTER
- PHARAOH'S DAUGHTER'S SERVANT
- MOSES
- ISRAELITE SLAVE (nonspeaking)

- EGYPTIAN SLAVE MASTER
- AARON
- PHARAOH
- PHARAOH'S SERVANT 1
- PHARAOH'S SERVANT 2
- PHARAOH'S SERVANT 3
- PLAGUE BRINGER
- ISRAELITE 1
- ISRAELITE 2
- ISRAELITE 3
- ISRAELITES (nonspeaking)
- PHARAOH'S ARMY (nonspeaking)

Presentation Suggestions

This play includes 9 scenes. The setting alternates between modern time and ancient Egypt. Consider decorating the back of the stage with small flags made by students. The SETTING at the beginning of each scene is to assist the characters and is not intended to be read. Performance suggestions (gestures, movements, facial expressions) and pronunciation helps are included in brackets.

Escape to Freedom

Scene 1—The Seder

SETTING: Modern time at the home of a Jewish family. Onstage are Narrator 1, Narrator 2, David, Sarah, Father Rosen, and Mother Rosen.

NARRATOR 1: Let's join the Rosen family in their home.

NARRATOR 2: It is time for the Jewish holiday called Passover.

NARRATOR 1: The family celebrates on the first night of the 8-day holiday with a special dinner.

NARRATOR 2: The dinner is called a **Passover Seder.**

[pronounced SAY-der]

MOTHER: Let's prepare the Seder plate for tonight's dinner. Sarah, spoon some horseradish on the plate.

DAVID: Horseradish tastes so hot and bitter!

SARAH: I don't like it either! Why do we have to have it on the plate at all, Mother?

MOTHER: It represents a time when our ancestors were slaves in Egypt. Its bitter taste reminds us of the harsh life.

DAVID: Our ancestors were slaves?

FATHER: Yes, the Egyptian Pharaoh forced the Israelites to do hard work for him.

SARAH: What kind of hard work?

FATHER: All kinds of work, but mostly making buildings.

MOTHER: See this charoset on our Seder plate?

[pronounced khah-roh-SEHT (the ch is pronounced like the ch in "Bach")]

DAVID: The ground fruit and nuts?

MOTHER: Yes, it represents mortar.

SARAH: What's mortar?

FATHER: It's like cement. The Israelites used it with the bricks to make buildings for Pharaoh.

DAVID: Tell us more about what life was like for the Israelites in Egypt.

Scene 2—The Israelites in Egypt

SETTING: Ancient Egypt. Onstage are Narrator 3, Narrator 4, Pharaoh's daughter, and her servant. At the end of the scene Moses, a slave, and an Egyptian master are onstage.

NARRATOR 3: About 3,250 years ago, many Israelites lived in Egypt.

NARRATOR 4: They were all part of one family—the distant descendants of Jacob.

NARRATOR 3: Long ago, Jacob and his twelve sons moved to Egypt.

NARRATOR 4: Jacob was also known by the name **Israel.**

NARRATOR 3: After many generations, that one family in Egypt was more than a million people.

NARRATOR 4: We call all of the members of that one family Israelites because they all descended from Jacob, who was called Israel.

NARRATOR 3: Pharaoh was worried that so many Israelites were a threat to his power.

NARRATOR 4: So Pharaoh made them slaves.

NARRATOR 3: One day Pharaoh ordered all first-born Israelite baby boys to be killed.

NARRATOR 4: But one Israelite mother hid her baby son in a basket on the river.

NARRATOR 3: Pharaoh's daughter found him.

PHARAOH'S DAUGHTER: Look! A baby in a basket.

SERVANT: Its blanket has an Israelite design on it.

PHARAOH'S DAUGHTER: It's an Israelite baby.

SERVANT: Its mother must have hid him to protect him.

PHARAOH'S DAUGHTER: So he wouldn't be killed by Pharaoh.

SERVANT: What a sweet baby.

PHARAOH'S DAUGHTER: I'll keep him and raise him as my own son.

SERVANT:	But your father…
PHARAOH'S DAUGHTER:	Shush! I'll name the baby Moses.
	[Pharaoh's daughter and her servant exit with the basket]
NARRATOR 3:	Moses was raised in Pharaoh's house.
NARRATOR 4:	But he knew he was an Israelite.
	[Moses enters and stands to one side. An Israelite slave and an Egyptian master enter.]
NARRATOR 3:	Moses didn't like how Pharaoh treated the other Israelites.
NARRATOR 4:	One day, he saw an Egyptian slave master beating a slave.
	[Egyptian pretending to whip the Israelite slave—slave pretending to be whipped]
MOSES:	Stop! Don't whip him!
EGYPTIAN:	Stay out of this!
MOSES:	Stop, I said!
	[Moses and the Egyptian struggle; the Egyptian falls to the floor]
NARRATOR 3:	Moses was so angry he killed the Egyptian.
NARRATOR 4:	Then Moses ran away from Egypt.

Scene 3—Back at the Rosen House

SETTING: Modern time back at the Rosen House. Onstage are Narrator 1, Narrator 2, David, Sarah, Father Rosen, and Mother Rosen.

NARRATOR 1:	Now we're back to the Rosen house.
NARRATOR 2:	David and Sarah are still helping prepare the Seder plate.
DAVID:	Now I understand why we eat the horseradish and the chopped fruit.
SARAH:	But why are parsley and hardboiled eggs on the Seder plate?
FATHER:	They represent the renewal of life in the springtime.
DAVID:	Because Passover is celebrated in the springtime?
MOTHER:	Yes, and they also represent the hope that life would be better.

SARAH: Then why do we dip the parsley and the eggs in this saltwater?

MOTHER: The saltwater represents the tears of the slaves.

FATHER: The saltwater also represents the water from the Red Sea.

DAVID: Tell us about the Red Sea.

Scene 4—Moses and Pharaoh, Part 1

SETTING: Ancient Egypt. Onstage are Narrator 3, Narrator 4, and Moses. Later present are Pharaoh, Aaron, Pharaoh's servant, and other servants. Walking onstage and exiting through this scene is the Plague Bringer. Onstage is a chair representing Pharaoh's throne.

NARRATOR 3:   After Moses ran away from Egypt he wandered in the desert.

[Moses wanders across the stage]

NARRATOR 4:   In the desert, God told Moses to return to Egypt and lead the Israelites out of Egypt.

NARRATOR 3:   God told Moses to tell Pharaoh to "Let my people go!"

NARRATOR 4:   So Moses went back to Egypt.

NARRATOR 3:   There Moses found his brother Aaron.

[Aaron enters from stage left or stage right; he and Moses wave, hug, or shake hands]

NARRATOR 4:   Together they went to see Pharaoh.

[Pharaoh enters from stage left or stage right with his servants; Pharaoh sits on his "throne"]

PHARAOH: Why have you returned, Moses?

MOSES: I've come to ask you to let the Israelites leave so they can worship God.

PHARAOH: No! They are my slaves.

AARON: God says to let them go.

PHARAOH: No!

MOSES: Then God will show you a sign of His power.

AARON: [Throws his staff on the ground; bends over and picks up a "snake"] See! God has turned my staff into a snake.

PHARAOH: I still won't let the slaves go.

MOSES:	Let the slaves go or God will turn the Nile River into blood.
PHARAOH:	No!
PLAGUE BRINGER:	[Walks across the stage with a glass filled with red paper. He holds it up for the audience to see] Water!
	[Plague Bringer then exits]
SERVANT:	Look! The water from the Nile has turned to blood.
PHARAOH:	I still won't let the slaves go.
MOSES:	Let the slaves go or God will fill Egypt with frogs.
PHARAOH:	No—they can't go!
PLAGUE BRINGER:	[Walks across stage tossing balls of crumpled green paper into the air] Frogs!
	[Plague Bringer exits]
PHARAOH'S SERVANTS:	Frogs! They're everywhere!
PHARAOH:	Okay! Okay! You can take the slaves! Just get rid of the frogs!
NARRATOR 3:	Moses and Aaron left.
NARRATOR 4:	God caused the frogs to die.

Scene 5—Moses and Pharaoh, Part 2

SETTING: Ancient Egypt. Onstage are Narrator 3, Narrator 4, Moses, Aaron, Pharaoh, and Pharaoh's servants. Walking onstage and exiting through this scene are the Plague Bringer and Pharaoh's Guard. Onstage is a chair representing Pharaoh's throne.

NARRATOR 3:	Pharaoh saw that the frogs were gone.
PHARAOH:	I've changed my mind!
MOSES:	Pharaoh—let the slaves go!
PHARAOH:	No!
MOSES:	Then the dust in Egypt will become gnats!
	[Aaron strikes the floor with his staff]
PLAGUE BRINGER:	[Enters from stage left or stage right, walks across stage tossing slips of black paper into the air] Gnats!
	[Plague Bringer exits]

[Pharaoh and Servants wave their hands to shoo away the gnats]

MOSES: And Egypt will be filled with flies!

PLAGUE BRINGER: [Walks across stage tossing more black paper into the air] Flies!

[Plague Bringer exits]

[Pharaoh and Servants wave their hands faster]

PHARAOH: Okay! Okay! You can take the slaves!

NARRATOR 3: God got rid of the gnats and the flies.

NARRATOR 4: So Pharaoh changed his mind again.

[Moses and Aaron start to leave]

PHARAOH: Wait! I've changed my mind!

MOSES: Let the slaves go or God will kill all your cattle, horses, camels, sheep, and goats.

PHARAOH: No way!

PLAGUE BRINGER: [Walks across the stage] Say "goodbye" to your animals!

[Plague Bringer exits. Offstage sounds of mooing, braying, baaing, and then a thud, followed by silence]

AARON: And God will cover your people and animals with painful sores.

PHARAOH: No way!

PLAGUE BRINGER: [Walks across the stage] Ouch!

[Plague Bringer exits]

[Servants hold onto parts of their bodies and moan]

MOSES: And God will send hail to destroy the crops.

PLAGUE BRINGER: [Walks across the stage tossing white slips of paper into the air] Hail!

[Plague Bringer exits]

PHARAOH'S SERVANT: It's hailing—right here in Egypt!

PHARAOH: Okay, stop! You can all go!

NARRATOR 1: But when God stopped the animals from dying, healed the sores, and stopped the hail. . .

NARRATOR 4: Pharaoh changed his mind AGAIN!

NARRATOR 3: Again?

NARRATOR 4: Yes! Again!

MOSES: Pharaoh, when are you going to learn?

AARON: God means business. Let His people go!

PHARAOH: How about if I just let the men go?

AARON: Not good enough.

MOSES: Too bad, Pharaoh. You had your chance.

AARON: Moses, let God do His thing.

[Moses holds out his staff]

PLAGUEBRINGER: [Walks across the stage tossing more black slips of paper into the air] Locusts!

[Plague Bringer then exits]

PHAROAH'S SERVANTS: [running around the stage and shouting] "Locusts! Everywhere!"

PHARAOH: More bugs! And they're eating all the plants.

MOSES: [Holds his staff out again] And darkness for three days!

PLAGUEBRINGER: [walks across stage, pretending not to be able to see] Where is everyone?

[Plague Bringer exits]

NARRATOR 3:   Once again Pharaoh said he'd let the slaves go.

NARRATOR 4:   And then he changed his mind again.

Scene 6—Back at the Rosen House

SETTING: Modern times at the Rosen house. Onstage are Narrator 1, Narrator 2, David, Sarah, Father Rosen, and Mother Rosen.

NARRATOR 1:   Let's return to the Rosen house.

NARRATOR 2:   Father is explaining the plagues.

DAVID: Pharaoh was sure dumb!

SARAH: Why didn't he just let them go after the first plague?

FATHER: God wanted to make sure Pharaoh knew He was serious.

DAVID: What do you mean?

FATHER: Every time God hardened Pharaoh's heart. . .

MOTHER: . . . it gave God another chance to show Pharaoh His power.

DAVID: You mean to prove that God was God?

SARAH:	And that the plagues weren't just coincidences?
FATHER:	That's right.
DAVID:	Well, Pharaoh should have figured it out by now!
MOTHER:	No, it took one more plague to convince him.
SARAH:	What was that plague?
FATHER:	The final plague is how we get the name of our holiday.

Scene 7—The Final Plague

SETTING: Ancient Egypt, outside Pharaoh's palace, with the Israelites. Onstage are Narrator 3, Narrator 4, Moses, Aaron, and a group of Israelites. At the end of the scene, Pharaoh enters.

NARRATOR 3:	Moses and Aaron left Pharaoh's palace.
NARRATOR 4:	Then God prepared to send a final plague.
AARON:	[Speaking to a group of Israelites] Listen everyone. There will be one more plague tonight.
ISRAELITE 1:	Another plague?
ISRAELITE 2:	You'd think God had already sent enough plagues.
ISRAELITE 3:	What more could God possibly do to change Pharaoh's heart?
MOSES:	God is sending an Angel of Death. . .
AARON:	. . . to kill all of the first-born sons living in Egypt.
ISRAELITE 1:	All first-born sons living in Egypt?
ISRAELITE 2:	But I have sons here in Egypt.
ISREALITE 3:	So do I. How do we protect our own sons?
AARON:	Kill a sheep and wipe its blood on your doorframe.
MOSES:	That will show the Angel of Death which houses belong to the Israelites.
ISRAELITE 1:	Then what?
AARON:	The Angel of Death will pass over those homes and not kill the sons inside.
	[Moses, Aaron, and the Israelites exit]
NARRATOR 3:	That night, the Angel of Death came to Egypt.

PLAGUE BRINGER: [Tiptoes across the stage and then exits]

NARRATOR 4: Pharaoh's own first-born son died.

NARRATOR 3: So did the other first-born sons in Egypt.

NARRATOR 4: All except for the Israelites, who had marked their doors with blood.

PHARAOH: [Walks on stage] Moses! Take your people and your animals and leave!

Scene 8—The Exodus

SETTING: Ancient Egypt, in the village. Onstage are Narrator 3, Narrator 4, Moses, Aaron, and Israelites. At the end of the scene, Pharaoh's soldiers and the Plague Maker are present.

NARRATOR 3: Pharaoh had finally agreed to let the Israelites leave Egypt.

NARRATOR 4: But Pharaoh had changed his mind before, so the people had to hurry.

NARRATOR 3: Just in case Pharaoh changed his mind again?

NARRATOR 4: Right.

MOSES: People! Get packed in a hurry!

AARON: Don't even let your dough rise before you bake your bread!

MOSES: Let's leave before Pharaoh changes his mind again.

NARRATOR 3: So the people packed and left Egypt.

[Moses, Aaron, and the Israelites carrying packages, wander across the stage and then exit]

NARRATOR 4: You'll never guess what happened then.

NARRATOR 3: Pharaoh didn't change his mind again, did he?

NARRATOR 4: Yes, he did! All of a sudden, he realized he no longer had all those slaves.

NARRATOR 3: But the Israelites had already left.

NARRATOR 4: Yes. So Pharaoh sent his army after them.

PHARAOH'S ARMY: [Enter stage left or stage right, march in a straight line across the stage, then exit]

NARRATOR 3:	Pharaoh's army chased the Israelites all the way to the Red Sea.
	[Moses and the Israelites enter from stage left or stage right]
NARRATOR 4:	When they got there…
	[Moses stretches out his staff]
ISRAELITE 1:	It sure is windy all of a sudden.
ISRAELITE 2:	It's God—He's drying up the water.
ISRAELITE 3:	Look! We can walk right through where the sea was.
NARRATOR 3:	So the Israelites crossed the Red Sea on dry ground.
	[Moses and the Israelites walk to the other side of the stage and stop]
PHARAOH'S ARMY:	[Marches onstage and stops halfway]
NARRATOR 4:	Then God did His thing again.
	[Moses stretches his staff out over the Red Sea again]
PLAGUE BRINGER:	[Carries a sheet of red fabric or paper across the stage] Water, water everywhere!
	[Plague Bringer then exits]
PHARAOH'S ARMY:	[Exits, pretending to swim]
NARRATOR 3:	Pharaoh's army was swallowed up in the water.
NARRATOR 4:	But the Israelites were safe.

Scene 9—The Rosen House

SETTING: Modern times back at the Rosen house. Onstage are Narrator 1, Narrator 2, David, Sarah, Father Rosen, and Mother Rosen.

NARRATOR 1:	Let's return to the Rosen house…
NARRATOR 2:	…and learn more about Passover.
SARAH:	So it's called "Passover" because the Angel of Death *passed over* the homes of the Israelites.
FATHER:	Yes.
DAVID:	And this lamb bone on the Seder plate?

MOTHER:	It's to remind us of the blood of the lamb that was used to mark the homes.
DAVID:	What about these crackers?
MOTHER:	They're called matzo bread.
SARAH:	It doesn't look like bread.
MOTHER:	It is made without the yeast that makes other bread fluffy.
DAVID:	Oh! So we eat it because the Israelites didn't take time to let their bread rise.
FATHER:	They left in a hurry.
DAVID:	Pharaoh sure wasn't very smart.
SARAH:	He should have let the Israelites go right away.
FATHER:	God didn't want to make it too easy on Pharaoh or on the Israelites.
MOTHER:	Sometimes lessons mean more if they're harder.
NARRATOR 1:	Jewish people celebrate Passover every year.
NARRATOR 2:	To remember their history.
NARRATOR 1:	To be thankful.
NARRATOR 2:	And to celebrate freedom.

FOLLOW-UP ACTIVITIES

Where in the World Am I? (Geography)

Find Israel on a world map. Locate the major rivers, mountains, and cities in Israel; find the longitudinal and latitudinal boundaries of modern-day Israel. Trace the paths of the Nile River and the Jordan River.

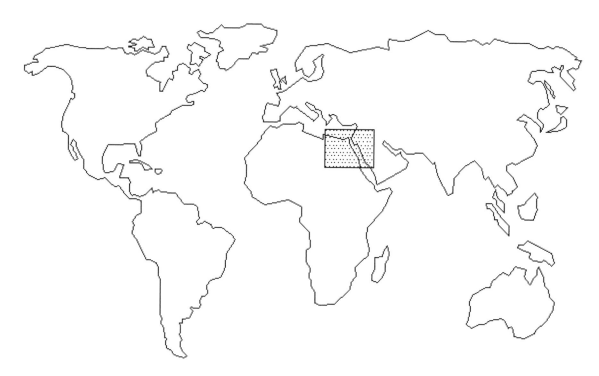

Make a Flag of Israel (Math, Art)

The flag of Israel includes many symbols. The star in the center of the flag is called the Star of David, which has been a Jewish symbol for hundreds of years. King David was one of the greatest kings of ancient Israel. The two blue strips along the top and bottom of the flag represent the pattern of the *tallit*, a shawl worn by Jewish people during prayer. To make an Israeli flag you will need:

- ❖ Sheet of 9-inch by 12-inch white construction paper
- ❖ Sheet of 9-inch by 12-inch blue construction paper
- ❖ Scissors
- ❖ Ruler
- ❖ Pencil
- ❖ Blue marking pen
- ❖ Glue

Using the ruler, pencil, and scissors, measure, mark, and cut the white paper to a size 8 inches by 11 inches. Then measure, mark, and cut two strips of blue paper 3 inches wide and 11 inches long. NOTE: The blue strips can be made ahead of time, using a paper cutter.

Place the white paper in front of you horizontally. Measure 2 inches from the top of the paper and mark with a pencil. Measure 2 inches from the bottom of the paper and mark with a pencil. Glue a 3-inch by 11-inch blue strip onto the white paper horizontally, at each of the 2-inch marks.

The Star of David is made from 2 equilateral triangles of the same size, each with 3 equal angles and 3 sides of equal length. One triangle is inverted over the other to create a star pattern. Following the illustration, use a ruler and a blue marker to draw a 3-inch star in the center of the white section of paper. Discuss different types of triangles and the concept of **parallelism**.

The ratio of the Israeli flag is 8:11 (width to length), so some measurements in this activity are approximate. Recalculate the measurements to make a larger or smaller flag.

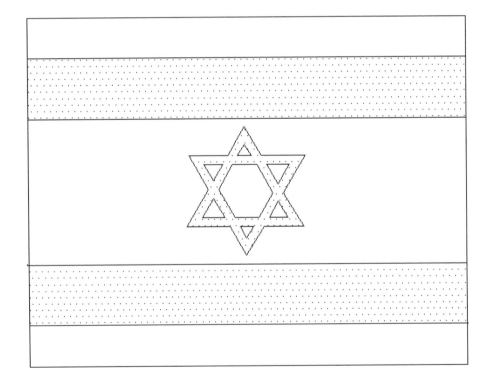

National Anthem of Israel (Literacy, Geography, Music)

The national anthem of Israel is called "Ha Tikvah," which is Hebrew for "The Hope." The word **Hebrew** means, "to cross over." It refers to the Israelites, after leaving Egypt, crossing over the Jordan River from the desert into the land promised by God. Check the library or look online for a recording of the music. The following are the words to "The Hope."

> As long as the Jewish spirit is yearning deep in the heart,
> With eyes turned toward the East, looking toward Zion,
> Then our hope—the 2000-year-old hope—will not be lost.
> To be a free people in our land,
> The land of Zion and Jerusalem.

Currency Conversion (Math)

The currency of Israel is the shekel [pronounced SHEH-kul]. Using an online currency converter or the financial section of a newspaper, compare one shekel with one US dollar. Calculate how much different items would cost in shekels, compared to dollars. Calculate how many shekels it would cost to buy:

❖ A candy bar (at US $.50)

❖ A pizza (at US $10.00)

❖ A car (at US $15,000.00)

HAVE A PASSOVER CELEBRATION

Celebrate Passover. The word **Seder** means, "order." The Seder meal is eaten on the first night of the 8-day Passover celebration. Usually the meal consists of matzo ball soup; roast chicken, lamb, or pot roast; and vegetables. An extra place is usually set at the table for the spirit of the Hebrew prophet Elijah, who is invited to attend. The following items are traditionally placed on a Passover Seder plate:

❖ Matzo (bread made without yeast)

❖ Bitter herbs (celery or parsley) and horseradish—to remember the bitterness of slavery; greenery suggests springtime renewal

❖ Sweet charoset—represents mortar

❖ Roasted bone of a lamb—reminder of the lambs sacrificed at Passover

❖ Hard-boiled eggs dipped in salt water—joy can come after sorrow

❖ Salt water—to represent the tears of captivity and the Red Sea

Charoset Recipe (Math)

Charoset is part of the Passover meal and is placed on the Seder plate. It represents the mortar (like cement) that the Israelites used when building with bricks while they were slaves in Egypt. Its sweetness symbolizes freedom after the bitterness of slavery. To make 2 cups of charoset you will need:

❖ 1 cup chopped nuts

❖ 5 apples, cored and finely chopped

❖ 1 teaspoon grated lemon peel

❖ 3 tablespoons lemon juice

❖ 2 tablespoons sugar

❖ 2 teaspoons cinnamon

❖ ¼ teaspoon ground ginger

❖ Finely chopped candied fruit or dates, if desired

❖ Bowl with cover

❖ Mixing spoon

Wash hands before cooking. Mix all ingredients in the bowl. Cover and refrigerate. Mound the charoset in the center of the Seder plate. Consider doubling the recipe and include the recalculations as a classroom math activity.

Matzo Bread Recipe (Math)

When Pharaoh decided to let the Israelites leave Egypt, they had to hurry, in case he changed his mind. So they baked their bread quickly, without spending the time to let the dough rise. Matzo represents this bread. It can be bought at most grocery stores, or you can make it yourself. To make 4 pieces of matzo you will need:

❖ 2 cups flour

❖ ½ cup cold water

❖ Mixing bowl

❖ Fork; floured rolling pin

❖ Additional flour for rolling

❖ Ungreased baking sheet

❖ Potholder

❖ Wide metal spatula

❖ Cooling rack

Wash hands before cooking. Preheat oven to 500 degrees. Place the flour and water in a large mixing bowl. Use the fork or clean fingers to mix the flour and water into dough. Divide into 4 equal pieces. Knead one piece of dough on a floured surface for about 2 minutes. Then, with floured rolling pin roll the dough into a flat piece about inch thick. Sprinkle with additional flour as needed to prevent dough from sticking to the surface or rolling pin.

Pierce the dough with the fork to make tiny holes that prevent it from buckling as it bakes. Roll the dough around the floured rolling pin to transfer it to the baking sheet. Spread it flat. Bake for 10 minutes, or until the edges begin to curl and brown spots appear on the surface. Remove from oven. Using the wide spatula, turn the matzo over. Return it to the oven and bake for an additional 8 minutes, or until brown. Remove from oven. Transfer the baked matzo onto a cooling rack. Repeat for the other pieces of dough.

Double or triple the recipe and recalculate the measurements as a classroom math activity.

Frogs (Math, Art)

Make origami frogs as props for the play. For each frog you will need one sheet of 8½ by 11 inch sheet of thin green paper. NOTE: Construction paper will be too thick to fold. As students are making frogs, discuss geometric shapes—creating squares from rectangular sheets of paper and creating triangles from squares. NOTE: Dotted lines in illustrations represent the location of folds or the next place to fold paper to.

Fold your rectangular sheet of paper diagonally so that the top edge lines up with the side edge. Then cut or carefully fold and tear off the remaining edge, leaving a square.

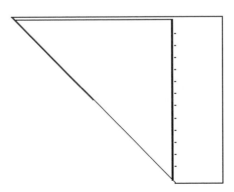

Lay the paper flat and refold it diagonally in the other direction. Open it flat again and fold it in half in both directions. Open it flat again so the fold creases now look like this:

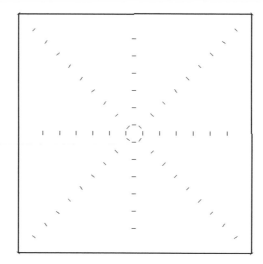

Push in on the center edges while folding the top edge down to meet the bottom edge. You will end up with a triangle.

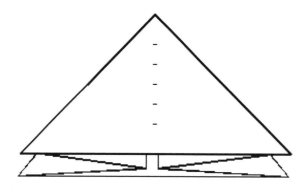

With the open end of the triangle toward you, take the lower right corner of the TOP layer and fold it up along the dotted line to meet the top point of the triangle. Repeat with the lower left corner. Your frog will now look like this.

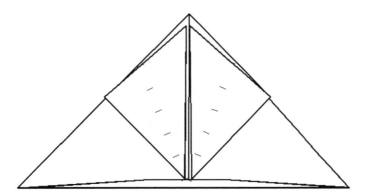

Now fold the edge of the right inner triangle toward the center at the dotted line. Do the same with the edge of the left inner triangle, so that it looks like this.

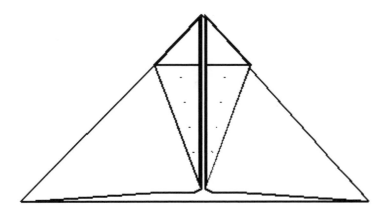

Now fold both the new top layer along with the layer beneath it outward along the dotted lines like this.

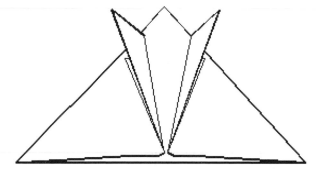

Turn your frog over. It should look like this.

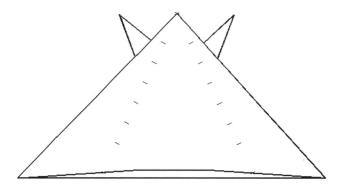

Fold the right edge down toward the center.

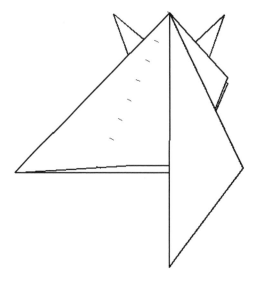

Then do the same on the left side.

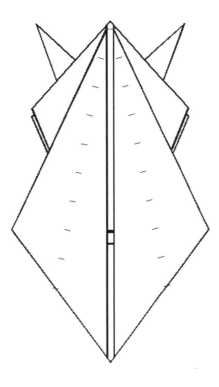

Fold the frog in the middle at the dotted line shown in the next drawing.

The frog's back feet should now be underneath its body and next to its head. Fold the lower section of its body (about ½ inch) at the dotted line in the next drawing.

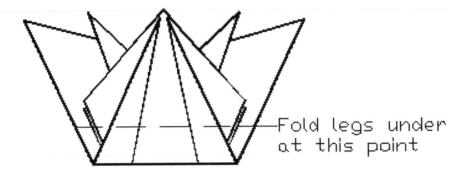

Fold legs under at this point

After the last fold, the frog should now look like this, with his feet behind him.

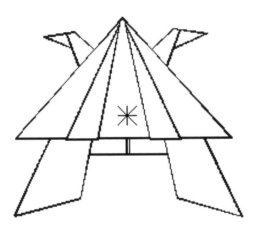

Place your frog on a hard surface. Press on the end of its back (at the star) and slide your finger off the frog to release him into the air.

Timeline (Math, History)

Discuss the Jewish calendar that dates history from the creation of the world. Our year AD 2000 is the Jewish year 5760. Refer to the discussion in the chapter entitled **Timelines and Number Lines.** Using the equation 2000 = 5760, determine other events in history and calculate their year on the Jewish timeline. Here are a few suggestions:

- ❖ Columbus' voyage (1492)
- ❖ Declaration of Independence (1776)
- ❖ Your birth year
- ❖ This year

SUGGESTIONS FOR FURTHER ACTIVITIES

History: Research ancient Egyptian history. Assuming the Israelites left Egypt in approximately 1250 BC (according to our calendar), determine what else was happening at that time in Egypt and in the rest of the world.

Social Studies: Discuss what freedom means and how slavery has existed everywhere in the world throughout history. Discuss the importance of freedom for all people.

Language Arts: Have students write a poem or story about freedom.

Science: Discuss a lunar month and how it relates to a month of our calendar. (See the chapter entitled **Calendars.**)

Science: Compare a Jewish week, in which days begin at sunset, to days in the western world, which are determined as beginning at midnight.

Science: Israelites left Egypt to go to the land God promised them—a land "flowing with milk and honey." Research bees and how they make honey.

Math: Discuss the differences between the Jewish lunar calendar and the solar calendar, including why a thirteenth month is added to the Jewish calendar every few years to keep it in line with the solar year. Discuss and compare this additional thirteenth month with our leap year, in which we add an extra day (February 29) every four years.

Art Appreciation: Find a picture of Leonardo Da Vinci's painting, *The Last Supper.* This artwork depicts the most famous Passover Seder in art history. Discuss the artistic style of Leonardo Da Vinci.

May—May Day

(England, Scotland, France, Italy, Germany, Russia, USA)

BACKGROUND

The celebration of May Day began in ancient times. Many countries in Europe celebrated the first of May as the end of winter and the beginning of spring. New grass and flowers played an important part in the celebration.

READERS THEATRE SCRIPT—THE MERRY MONTH OF MAY

Suggested Costumes and Props

- ❖ Telephones (Scene 2)
- ❖ Yellow block or box to represent cheese (Scene 3)
- ❖ Empty carton or bottle of milk (Scene 3)
- ❖ Box to represent cookies (Scene 3)
- ❖ Flowers in bunches and garlands (Scene 4)
- ❖ American flag (Scene 5)

Characters

The following is a list of characters. The May Day party has been divided into three scenes to allow for more readers to participate as different Narrators.

- NARRATOR 1
- NARRATOR 2
- JAN
- BRYAN
- GREG

- DELINDA
- CARLOS
- IVAN
- RENEE

Presentation Suggestions

This play includes 5 scenes. Narrator 1, Narrator 2, Jan, and Bryan are onstage at all times. The other characters join them in Scenes 2, 3, 4, and 5. Consider decorating the back of the stage with a large flag from one of the countries discussed in the play, with the smaller French flags made by students, or with plastic vines and flowers. The **SETTING** at the beginning of each scene is to assist the characters and is not intended to be read. Performance suggestions (gestures, movements, facial expressions) and pronunciation helps are included in brackets.

The Merry Month of May

Scene 1—May Day Morning

SETTING: Modern time. Onstage are Narrator 1, Narrator, and two friends—Jan and Bryan.

NARRATOR 1:	The day is May first.
NARRATOR 2:	The time is now.
JAN:	May is a merry month!
BRYAN:	Who's Mary?
JAN:	Not Mary—the girl. Merry—like happy!
BRYAN:	Happy?
JAN:	Yes, happy—like how you say "Merry Christmas."
BRYAN:	And "Merry Birthday"?
JAN:	You know what I mean! The word "merry" means happy.
BRYAN:	So you're saying May is a happy month?
JAN:	Yes.
BRYAN:	What's so happy about it?
JAN:	Well, it's spring.
BRYAN:	But spring starts in March, not May.
JAN:	You're right. But May is close to summer.
BRYAN:	Summer doesn't start until June.
JAN:	Yes, but…
BRYAN:	There aren't even any good holidays in May.
JAN:	There's May Day.
BRYAN:	What's May Day?
JAN:	It's the first day of May.
BRYAN:	So what? Every month has a first day.
JAN:	But May first is special.
BRYAN:	What's special about May first?
JAN:	It's a time for celebration.

BRYAN:	Celebration?
JAN:	Yep!
BRYAN:	As in party?
JAN:	Yep!
BRYAN:	When do we start?

Scene 2—The Invitations

SETTING: Later that day. Onstage throughout the scene are Narrator 1, Narrator 2, Jan, and Bryan. Their friends enter stage left or stage right, read their lines, and exit.

NARRATOR 1:	Jan and Bryan decided to have a May Day party.
NARRATOR 2:	They phoned their friends to invite them.
NARRATOR 1:	Each person was told to find out one thing about May Day.
NARRATOR 2:	. . . and share it at the party.
	[Greg enters from stage left or stage right]
JAN:	[on the phone] Greg, we're having a May Day party.
GREG:	[on the phone] Great! What shall I bring?
JAN:	[on the phone] Pick a country and bring something people would have used there to celebrate May Day.
GREG:	[on the phone] I'll be there!
	[Greg exits]
	[Delinda enters from stage left or stage right]
BRYAN:	[on the phone] Delinda, we're having a May Day party.
DELINDA:	[on the phone] What's a May Day party?
BRYAN:	[on the phone] I have no idea—but find out and bring something people use to celebrate.
DELINDA:	[on the phone] Okay!
	[Delinda exits]
	[Carlos enters from stage left or stage right]
JAN:	[on the phone] Carlos, we're having a May Day party.
CARLOS:	[on the phone] That sounds like fun! I know just what to bring.
JAN:	[on the phone] Terrific! See you.

[Carlos exits]

[Ivan enters from stage left or stage right]

BRYAN: [on the phone] Ivan, we're having a May Day party.

IVAN: [on the phone] Wow! Can I come?

BRYAN: [on the phone] You mean you know what May Day is?

IVAN: [on the phone] Sure. My grandpa told me about how he celebrated May Day in Russia.

BRYAN: [on the phone] Then bring something to share.

IVAN: [on the phone] Okay—see you.

[Ivan exits]

[Renee enters from stage left or stage right]

JAN: [on the phone] Renee, would you like to come to our May Day party?

RENEE: [on the phone] Yes! I'll bring something special.

JAN: [on the phone] See you.

[Renee exits]

NARRATOR 1: Jan and Bryan finished making their phone calls.

JAN: I think we've invited everyone.

BRYAN: What shall I bring?

JAN: You've got the most important job.

BRYAN: What's that?

JAN: Let me tell you.

[Jan and Bryan exit]

NARRATOR 1: I wonder what Jan told Bryan.

NARRATOR 2: I guess we'll have to go to the party and find out.

Scene 3—The Party

SETTING: Later that day at the party. Onstage are Narrator 1, Narrator 2, Jan, Bryan, and their friends.

NARRATOR 1: Everyone worked hard learning about May Day.

NARRATOR 2: Soon it was time for the party.

[The guests enter from stage left or stage right. Jan and Bryan welcome them.]

JAN: Thanks for coming, everyone!

BRYAN: Merry May Day!

RENEE: Mary couldn't come.

BRYAN: Not Mary, the girl. Merry, as in happy!

IVAN: Oh, Merry May Day!

JAN: Greg, what did you bring to celebrate May Day?

GREG: My grandparents were from England, so I brought cheese!

BRYAN: What does cheese have to do with May Day?

GREG: In May all the new grasses started to grow.

JAN: Because it was springtime?

GREG: Yes, and the cows had been inside the barn all winter.

BRYAN: So?

GREG: So in springtime, the farmers let the cows out in the field to eat the new grass.

BRYAN: But what does cheese have to do with it?

GREG: When the cows ate the grass, they made more milk.

JAN: So the farmers made cheese out of the extra milk!

RENEE: Hey, that's what I brought.

JAN: You brought cheese, too?

RENEE: No, I brought milk to celebrate May Day.

BRYAN: Milk?

RENEE: Yes, in France, cows were also an important part of May Day.

JAN: How?

RENEE: People decorated the cows with flowers and walked them in parades.

JAN: But why did you bring milk?

BRYAN: Renee, please don't tell us you want us to make our own cheese!

RENEE: No. In France, they drank warm milk for good luck.

CARLOS: The milk will go great with what I brought.

JAN: Those look yummy! What are they?

CARLOS: They're called bannocks. They're cookies from Scotland.

BRYAN: There's a cross on top of each one.

CARLOS: Long ago, kids used to roll the bannocks down a hill. If they landed cross side down, it was bad luck.

BRYAN: Isn't it bad luck *any time* cookies roll on the ground?

JAN: Wait a minute, Carlos. Do you want us to roll our cookies down the driveway?

CARLOS: No. I thought we could just eat them!

BRYAN: Great idea! Milk and cookies for everyone!

Scene 4—More Partying

SETTING: Later at the party. All characters are onstage.

NARRATOR 1: Everyone seems to be having a good time at Jan and Bryan's party.

NARRATOR 2: Yes. Let's see what the other guests brought.

JAN: Those cookies were really good, Carlos.

CARLOS: And they went great with the milk Renee brought.

BRYAN: What did you bring, Delinda?

DELINDA: After I learned about May Day in England, I went a-maying.

GREG: A-maying? What does that mean?

DELINDA: It just means to gather flowers in May.

JAN: What kind of flowers did you bring?

DELINDA: They're Hawthorn flowers.

CARLOS: They're beautiful.

DELINDA: See how they're bunched together like they're in knots?

GREG: Yes.

DELINDA: There's an old May Day song about gathering knots of flowers.

IVAN: How does it go?

DELINDA: One line says, "Here we go gathering nuts in May."

CARLOS: I'm confused. Are you supposed to gather flowers or nuts?

DELINDA: Well, the word "nuts" is an old English word that really means "knots."

BRYAN: Oh, nutty knots and naughty nuts!

JAN: Bryan—you are a nutty nut!

BRYAN: Funny, Jan. So what did you bring?

JAN:	I brought flowers, too.
GREG:	Jan, your flowers really ARE tied together—all in a line.
JAN:	It's called a garland.
DELINDA:	What kind of vase would you use?
JAN:	They weren't put in a vase. They were used for hanging.
BRYAN:	For hanging what?
JAN:	In ancient Rome, people hung strings of flowers around the statue of Flora.
GREG:	Who was Flora?
JAN:	She was the Roman goddess of springtime.
RENEE:	It reminds me of a Hawaiian lei.
JAN:	Yes, it is like a lei.
BRYAN:	To say "Aloha! Hello, spring!"
IVAN:	I really hope you're not going to dance the hula, Bryan.
BRYAN:	Not now.
CARLOS:	So what did you bring, Ivan?
IVAN:	My grandfather came here from Russia.
JAN:	That's interesting. Did they have unusual flowers there?
IVAN:	I didn't bring any flowers.
GREG:	How did they celebrate May Day in Russia?
IVAN:	Russia was a communist nation when my grandfather lived there.
RENEE:	How did he celebrate May Day?
IVAN:	When Russia was communist, May Day was a holiday about workers.
JAN:	No flowers?
GREG:	No cheese?
RENEE:	No milk?
CARLOS:	No cookies?
NARRATOR 1:	I wonder how the Russian people celebrated May Day.
NARRATOR 2:	I wonder what Bryan brought.

Scene 5—Party On

SETTING: The party continues. All characters are onstage.

NARRATOR 1: What do you think Ivan brought to show how his grandfather celebrated May Day in Russia?

NARRATOR 2: Let's listen in and find out.

JAN: Everyone else brought something to show how other countries celebrate springtime.

GREG: Why did Russia celebrate workers?

IVAN: Because of something that happened in America.

JAN: What happened in America?

IVAN: On May first, 1886, a group of American workers went on strike.

GREG: What does that mean?

IVAN: It means they refused to work because they wanted better working conditions.

JAN: What happened?

IVAN: Several strikers and policemen were killed.

RENEE: That sounds awful!

GREG: How did it become a celebration?

IVAN: It became a time to remember workers.

DELINDA: To honor them?

IVAN: Yes.

JAN: So what did you bring then, Ivan?

IVAN: I brought an American flag.

GREG: Why a flag?

IVAN: So we would remember American workers.

RENEE: I thought we celebrate workers some other time of the year in America.

CARLOS: Yes, America celebrates workers in September.

IVAN: But a lot of the world celebrates workers on May Day. And it all started in America.

DELINDA: What did you bring, Bryan?

BRYAN: I brought something to celebrate like they do in England, France, Germany, and early America.

CARLOS:	What is it?
BRYAN:	[pointing] Ta-da!
CARLOS:	You brought a bald Christmas tree with no branches?
BRYAN:	Yes, but it's more than that.
IVAN:	It's a bald Christmas tree with a bunch of ribbons tied on top.
RENEE:	I know what that is! It's a Maypole!
BRYAN:	Yes!
DELINDA:	What's a Maypole?
BRYAN:	In many countries, people would circle around a pole in the center of town.
GREG:	Like dancing?
IVAN:	I think Bryan IS going to dance the hula.
BRYAN:	No, the hula is not the kind of dancing you do around a Maypole.
RENEE:	I'm not a very good dancer.
BRYAN:	Sometimes there was music, but sometimes people just walked around the Maypole.
CARLOS:	How do we do it?
BRYAN:	Everybody grab one of the ribbons. Boys face this way. Girls face that way.
JAN:	Okay, we've got our ribbons.
BRYAN:	Start walking — boys lift your ribbons up over the heads of the girls—girls go underneath the boys' ribbons.
JAN:	We're doing it!
	[Students walk in a circle for a while and then stop]
CARLOS:	Cows, cookies, flowers, workers, and Maypole dancing!
DELINDA:	I never knew May Day was so fun.
IVAN:	And celebrated so many ways in different countries.
BRYAN:	Well, I know my favorite part.
JAN:	What's that?
BRYAN:	The food!
JAN:	More cookies and milk for everyone!

FOLLOW-UP ACTIVITIES

Where in the World Am I? (Geography)

The following countries are referred to in the script: England, France, Germany, Russia, USA, Scotland, and Italy. Locate them on a world map and find their latitudinal and longitudinal boundaries. Locate the major rivers, mountains, and cities in the countries introduced.

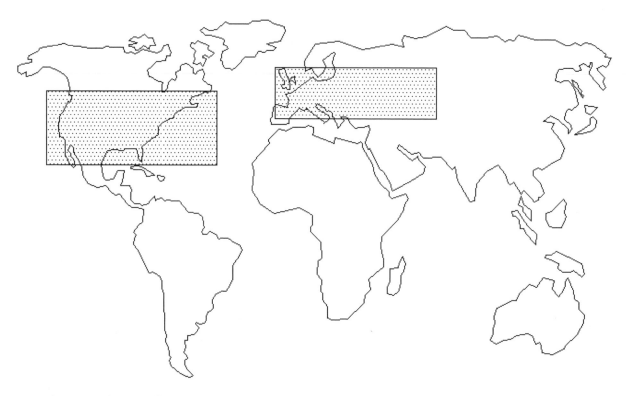

Make a Flag of France (Math, Art)

Students can make a flag from any or all of the countries referred to in the play, giving a report about the colors, symbolism, and history of the flag. Or all students can make a flag of France, using the following instructions. To make a French flag you will need:

- ❖ One sheet of 9-inch by 12-inch white construction paper
- ❖ One sheet of 9-inch by 12-inch blue construction paper
- ❖ One sheet of 9-inch by 12-inch red construction paper
- ❖ Scissors
- ❖ Ruler
- ❖ Pencil
- ❖ Glue

The ratio of the French flag is 2:3 (width to length). With a ruler, pencil, and scissors, measure, mark, and cut the white construction paper to a size 8 inches by 12 inches. Then measure, mark, and cut the blue and the red construction paper into 3 equal pieces of 8 inches by 4 inches. NOTE: This step can be done ahead of time using a paper cutter. Since this is intended as a math activity, however, students are encouraged to work in pairs, one student measuring and cutting the blue paper and one student measuring and cutting the red paper.

Place the white construction paper in front of you horizontally. Glue an 8-inch by 4-inch piece of blue paper onto the left-hand edge of the white paper, matching edges. Glue an 8-inch by 4-inch piece of red paper onto the right-hand edge of the white paper, matching edges.

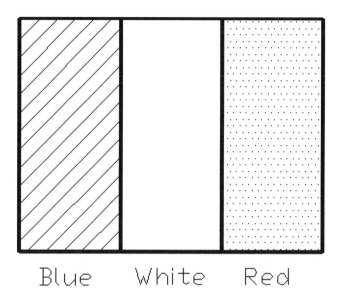

Blue   White   Red

Compare and contrast: the French flag (equal blue, white, and red vertical stripes), the Italian flag (equal green, white, and red vertical stripes), the Russian flag (equal white, blue and red horizontal stripes), and the German flag (equal black, red, and yellow horizontal stripes). Compare the color combinations of the flags of France, the United Kingdom, and the United States (all red, white, and blue).

National Anthem of Germany (Literacy, Music)

Read and discuss the lyrics of the national anthem of any or all of the countries presented in the play. Check the library or look online for recordings. The following are the lyrics for the national anthem of the Republic of Germany. Discuss the concepts and phrases in the national anthem—unity, right, freedom, flourish.

Unity and right and freedom
For the German fatherland;
Let us all pursue this purpose
Brotherly, with heart and hand.
Unity and right and freedom
Are the pledge of happiness.
Flourish in this blessing's glory,
Flourish, German fatherland.
Flourish in this blessing's glory,
Flourish, German fatherland.

Currency Conversion (Math)

Using an online currency converter or the financial section of a newspaper, look up the currencies of the countries referred to in the script: England and Scotland (pound); France, Germany, and Italy (euro); Russia (ruble). How does each currency compare to a US dollar? Calculate how much it would cost in each country's currency to buy:

- ❖ A candy bar (at US $.50)
- ❖ A pizza (at US $10.00)
- ❖ A car (at US $15,000.00)

HAVE A MAY DAY CELEBRATION

Celebrate May Day with a traditional English tea. Enjoy hot tea and toasted English muffins, or scones and jam. Or prepare English "treacle parkin" or Scottish "bannocks" ahead of time to share with the class. Serve the tea English style—hot, with sugar and cream. Or enjoy warm milk and cheese and think about the happy cows munching on tender new grass! Don't forget napkins, cups, plates (if needed), and utensils.

Treacle Parkin Recipe (Math)

To make one recipe of treacle parkin (serves approximately 12), you will need:

- ❖ 2 cups all-purpose flour
- ❖ 2 tablespoons ground ginger
- ❖ 1 tablespoon cinnamon
- ❖ 1½ cups packed dark brown sugar
- ❖ 1 cup unsalted butter, softened
- ❖ 1 cup molasses
- ❖ 2 eggs, beaten
- ❖ 1 teaspoon baking soda
- ❖ ½ cup scalded milk
- ❖ Powdered sugar
- ❖ Sifter
- ❖ 8- or 9-inch-square baking pan
- ❖ Electric mixer
- ❖ Rubber spatula
- ❖ 3 medium-sized mixing bowls
- ❖ Pan for scalding milk
- ❖ Measuring cups
- ❖ Measuring spoons

Wash hands before cooking. Preheat oven to 325. Grease and flour the baking pan. Sift flour, ginger, and cinnamon together into a bowl and set aside. Cream brown sugar and butter in a second bowl. Combine molasses and eggs in a third bowl, and add alternately with the dry ingredients into the sugar mixture.

Dissolve baking soda in hot milk. Stir into the batter. Pour batter into pan. Bake 90 minutes, or until done. Cool 10 minutes, remove from pan, and cool completely. Dust with powdered sugar and cut into slices.

Double the recipe and recalculate the new measurements. (Make sure to use 2 pans if doubling the recipe.) Refer to the chapter entitled **Measurements and Metric Conversions.**

Bannock Recipe (Math)

Scottish bannocks and English scones are quite similar. Often bannocks are shaped into one large circle and then sliced into four pie-shaped pieces. Sometimes dried fruit is added to the dough before cooking. Make Scottish bannocks for your May Day party. They can be made in the classroom using an electric frying pan. To make 6 to 8 small bannocks, you will need:

- ❖ 2 cups oatmeal

- ❖ 1 cup flour

- ❖ 1 teaspoon salt

- ❖ ¾ cup butter

- ❖ ½ cup hot water

- ❖ 2 tablespoons sugar

- ❖ Shortening for frying

- ❖ Mixing bowl

- ❖ 2 table knives or 1 pastry cutter

- ❖ Measuring cup

- ❖ Measuring spoons

- ❖ Wooden spoon

- ❖ Rolling pin

- ❖ Breadboard

- ❖ Extra flour for rolling

- ❖ Round cookie cutter

- ❖ Electric frying pan

- ❖ Spatula for turning

Wash hands before cooking. Mix dry ingredients in bowl. Cut the butter into the dry ingredients with the knives or pastry cutter until the mixture is like coarse breadcrumbs. Add water and mix into a dough. Using extra flour as needed, roll the dough until it is about ½ inch thick. Cut into rounds about 2 or 3 inches in diameter.

Fry in the greased electric frying pan until light brown. Turn and cook on the other side.

Each recipe makes 6 to 8 bannocks. Refer to the chapter entitled **Measurements and Metric Conversions,** and recalculate the recipe to make more servings for the class.

May Dance (Math, Physical Education, Music)

Attach long ribbons to the top of a tetherball pole (if possible, remove the ball). Stand in a circle around the pole, alternating boy–girl, each student holding a ribbon. Boys face one direction; girls face the other. Boys circle in one direction; girls the other. As they walk, boys raise their ribbons high and girls go beneath them.

Alternative 1: With joined hands held high, students form an archway that others walk or dance under.

Alternative 2: Students can participate in a May Day procession as done in ancient Europe, where villagers carried baskets of flowers or wreaths around the village. Students could march in procession around the playground, to other classrooms, or to a local park, stopping at various places to decorate or hand out flowers.

Alternative 3: Instead of interweaving ribbons around the Maypole, simply dance around the Maypole (decorated tetherball pole or basketball post) without ribbons. Do the dance in sets of 8 students, with four couples at each corner around the Maypole. Partners bow or curtsy to each other for 4 counts. Students then bow or curtsy to the opposite partner for 4 counts. All 8 students form a circle and side-step once around the circle to the right, returning to their original place. All students then side-step once around the circle to the left, returning to their original place. Students then join up with their partner and promenade (walk together) to the right, returning to their original place. This pattern can be repeated for as long as the music lasts. Use music with a lively beat—a 4-4 reel, a formal waltz, or English folk music.

May Baskets (Math, Art, Community Service)

Make May baskets. Decorate paper lunch bags or shoeboxes and fill them with flowers, drawings, candies, cookies, and small gifts. Deliver them to lower grade classrooms, to the school office staff, or to other teachers. Or choose an organization in the community, such as a nursing home or hospital, and arrange for their delivery. Or take them home to family members. Or exchange them at the classroom May Day celebration, like Valentines.

Springy Poetry (Language Arts)

Have students write a poem about May Day. The following may be used for inspiration:

Let's Rhyme with May

Give students a writing prompt, such as "We celebrate the month of May" and have them write a poem about May Day. The following words may help with rhyming inspiration:

bay	day	gay	jay	hey	hay	lay
clay	play	slay	sleigh	neigh	nay	pay
ray	bray	fray	gray	spray	stay	stray
say	they	weigh	way	okay	croquet	payday
weekday	midday	someday	sundae	ballet	buffet	Sunday
Monday	Tuesday	Wednesday	Thursday	Friday	Saturday	tray
halfway	driveway	pathway	everyday	Milky Way	anyway	holiday

Planting Flowers (Science)

Get into the swing of spring by growing flowers. Provide plastic cups for each student. Fill the cups with soil and seeds. Water the soil and place the plantings near a window.

Alternatively, purchase bedding plants or seeds and plant them in the schoolyard or near the office. Have students check and tend the plants regularly and keep "lab notes" on their progress.

SUGGESTED IDEAS FOR FURTHER ACTIVITIES

Social Studies: Research customs and beliefs regarding Hawaiian Lei Day, where people give each other flower leis. This centuries-old tradition became an official observance in 1928.

Science: Discuss the position of the sun and earth at springtime and how that affects the seasons and the growing of new plants. Discuss why May Day is such a traditional celebration of springtime. (See the chapter entitled **Calendars.**)

Science: Take a notebook and pencil to the park or playground. See who can come up with the longest list of "evidence of spring" (new sprouts, flowers, bird eggs, young animals, etc.)

Science: Research the Hawthorn flower. Locate where it grows in the world, what the plant looks like, and what type of climate it needs. Discuss reasons it might be an important part of a May Day celebration in England.

Science: Research how cheese is made, what cheeses are made from the milk of different animals (cows, goats, and buffalo, for example), and how the curing process creates different flavors of cheese. Bring in samples of different cheeses for tasting.

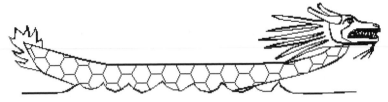

June—Dragon Boat Festival

(China)

BACKGROUND

There were many empires in the land that is now China before it was united under Emperor Chin. One empire was ruled by Emperor Chu, who had an advisor named Chu Yuan. There are many stories about Chu Yuan. Some say that other advisors were jealous of Chu Yuan and plotted against him, causing the Emperor to send Chu Yuan into exile. Other stories tell that the Emperor failed to follow Chu Yuan's advice, which resulted in the Emperor's death. In all versions, Chu Yuan wandered the countryside, writing poems about his country and feeling sad that he couldn't save the empire. In the end, Chu Yuan threw himself into the Mi-Lo River to end his suffering.

The Festival of the Dragon Boats recreates the villagers' attempt to save Chu Yuan and celebrates his service and love for his country. The festival became an annual celebration in China in approximately 227 BC. It is celebrated on the day of Chu Yuan's death—the fifth day of the fifth lunar month. Because a lunar month does not coincide with our solar calendar, the festival does not fall on the same day each year. It is generally celebrated sometime between April and June.

READERS THEATRE SCRIPT— SEARCHING FOR CHU YUAN

Suggested Costumes and Props

- ❖ Chair to represent Emperor Chu's throne (Scene 1)
- ❖ Armor for the warriors to wear—2 pieces of cardboard tied at the shoulder and waist with string (Scene 2)
- ❖ Swords, using yardsticks (Scene 2)
- ❖ Drums—boxes or upside-down buckets, played with the hand or a short stick. (Scenes 4 and 7)

102

❖ Dragon heads (see follow-up activity) and crepe paper streamers for boats (Scene 7)

❖ Crumpled white paper to simulate rice packets. (Scene 4)

Characters

The following is a list of characters. Nonspeaking roles include warriors, drummers, boat rowers, and villagers.

- NARRATOR 1
- NARRATOR 2
- CHU YUAN
- EMPEROR CHU
- CHIN AND CHU WARRIORS (nonspeaking)
- CITIZEN 1
- CITIZEN 2
- FISHERMAN 1

- FISHERMAN 2
- FISHERMAN 3
- FISHERMAN 4
- DRUMMER (nonspeaking)
- VILLAGER 1
- VILLAGER 2
- VILLAGER 3
- VILLAGER 4

Presentation Suggestions

This play includes 7 scenes. Narrator 1 and Narrator 2 will be onstage at all times. Consider decorating the back of the stage with a backdrop—made from butcher paper—depicting the Mi-Lo River, or with individual flags made by students. The **SETTING** at the beginning of each scene is to assist the characters and is not intended to be read. Performance suggestions (gestures, movements, facial expressions) and pronunciation helps are included in brackets.

Searching for Chu Yuan

Scene 1—The Royal Palace

SETTING: The royal palace of Emperor Chu, about 2300 years ago. Onstage are Narrator 1, Narrator 2, Chu Yuan, and Emperor Chu, who sits on his throne.

NARRATOR 1:	Our story begins in ancient China.
NARRATOR 2:	The time is almost 2300 years ago.
NARRATOR 1:	At that time there was a poet.
NARRATOR 2:	His name was Chu Yuan.
NARRATOR 1:	Chu Yuan was an advisor to Emperor Chu.
NARRATOR 2:	Chu Yuan loved his country very much.
CHU YUAN:	[bowing to the Emperor] Emperor Chu—I beg you not to meet with Emperor Chin!
EMPEROR CHU:	Why, Chu Yuan?
CHU YUAN:	Chin is a powerful warrior.
EMPEROR CHU:	That's why I must go see him—because he threatens our country.
CHU YUAN:	Emperor Chin's army might take over our country while you are gone.
EMPEROR CHU:	You have always served me well.
CHU YUAN:	Then follow my advice, Emperor.
EMPEROR CHU:	Not this time, Chu Yuan. I shall go meet with Chin.
CHU YUAN:	Please don't go!
EMPEROR CHU:	If I meet with Chin, maybe we can stop this war.
CHU YUAN:	[bows away from the Emperor and exits]
EMPEROR CHU:	Yes, I shall go meet with Emperor Chin.

From *Around the World Through Holidays: Cross Curricular Readers Theatre* written and illustrated by Carol Peterson. Westport, CT: Teacher Ideas Press/Libraries Unlimited. Copyright © 2006.

Scene 2—The Fall of the Empire

SETTING: The empire of Emperor Chin. Narrator 1, Narrator 2, Emperor Chu, and Emperor Chin's warriors are onstage. Later Citizen 1, Citizen 2, Emperor Chin's warriors, Emperor Chu's warriors, and Chu Yuan enter.

NARRATOR 1: Emperor Chu went to meet Emperor Chin.

NARRATOR 2: He wanted to stop the war.

NARRATOR 1: But Emperor Chin did not listen to Emperor Chu.

NARRATOR 2: Instead, Emperor Chu was captured by Emperor Chin's warriors.

EMPEROR CHU: I should have listened to Chu Yuan!

EMPEROR CHIN'S WARRIORS: [Grasp Chu by the wrists and take him off stage]

EMPEROR CHU: [offstage—yelling followed by silence]

NARRATOR 1: Emperor Chu died.

NARRATOR 2: Then Emperor Chin's army invaded.

EMPEROR CHIN'S WARRIORS: [march onstage from stage left or right]

CITIZEN 1: [enters from stage left or stage right] Chin has invaded!

EMPEROR CHU'S WARRIORS: [enter from stage left or stage right]

NARRATOR 1: There was war!

[Emperor Chin's warriors and Emperor Chu's warriors battle. Emperor Chin's warriors win]

NARRATOR 2: Chin's army conquered the capital city of Chu.

CITIZEN 2: [enters from stage left or stage right] Our country is lost!

NARRATOR 1: Chu Yuan felt he had failed his country.

CHU YUAN: If only I could have convinced Emperor Chu to follow my advice.

CITIZEN 1 and CITIZEN 2: Chu Yuan—We lost!

CHU YUAN: What am I to do?

NARRATOR 2: Emperor Chin united many empires into one.

NARRATOR 1: It was a time of change for the people of Chu.

NARRATOR 2: And a time of sadness for Chu Yuan.

Scene 3—Wandering

SETTING: The ancient countryside of China. Onstage are Narrator 1, Narrator 2, Chu Yuan, Villager 1, Villager 2, Villager 3, and Villager 4.

NARRATOR 1: Chu Yuan spent many years wandering the countryside.

[Chu Yuan enters from stage left or stage right and wanders across the stage]

NARRATOR 2: He couldn't stop feeling sad about his country.

NARRATOR 1: So he wrote poems about how much he loved his country.

NARRATOR 2: Everywhere he went, people asked him to tell them a poem.

VILLAGER 1: Tell us a poem, Chu Yuan!

VILLAGER 2: Yes, a poem about our country.

CHU YUAN: The thunder rumbles and the rain darkens;

The gibbons mourn, howling all the night;

The wind whistles and the trees are bare.

I am thinking of the young lord; I sorrow in vain.

VILLAGER 3: That's beautiful!

VILLAGER 4: But it's sad.

VILLAGER 1: Yes, it's really sad.

VILLAGER 2: Really sad and beautiful.

VILLAGER 3: Can't you write a happy poem, Chu Yuan?

CHU YUAN: No, I can't write happy poems.

VILLAGER 4: Why are you so sad?

CHU YUAN: I'm sad because I could not save our country.

Scene 4—Chu Yuan's Death

SETTING: Some time later; a fishing village along the Mi-Lo River in China. Onstage are Narrator 1, Narrator 2, Fisherman 1, Fisherman 2, Fisherman 3, and Fisherman 4. Fishermen sit in chairs or on the floor as if in a long boat, pretending to row. One drummer in the "boat" beats a drum with his hand or a short stick, where indicated.

NARRATOR 1:	One day Chu Yuan traveled to a village on the Mi-Lo River.
NARRATOR 2:	The villagers were fishing from their boats.
FISHERMAN 1:	[pointing offstage] Who's that by the edge of the river?
FISHERMAN 2:	He looks familiar.
FISHERMAN 3:	I know who that is!
FISHERMAN 4:	He's the poet Chu Yuan.
FISHERMAN 1:	Look! Chu Yuan jumped into the water!
CHU YUAN:	[pretends to jump in the water and lies down on the floor]
FISHERMAN 2:	Let's save him! (fishermen paddle faster)
FISHERMAN 3:	Where is he?
FISHERMAN 4:	Maybe the evil water spirit has taken him.
FISHERMAN 1:	Let's beat our drum.
FISHERMAN 2:	Yes, maybe the noise will frighten away the water spirit.
	[Drummers beat the drum while rowers continue to row. Then they stop drumming and rowing]
FISHERMAN 3:	I still don't see him.
FISHERMAN 4:	I hope the fish don't eat him!
FISHERMAN 1:	The fish are pretty hungry today.
FISHERMAN 2:	Let's throw our rice packets into the water.
FISHERMAN 3:	Maybe the fish will eat the rice…
FISHERMAN 4:	…instead of Chu Yuan.
	[Fishermen pretend to toss rice packets into the water]
NARRATOR 1:	But Chu Yuan's body was never found.
NARRATOR 2:	He died on the fifth day of the fifth lunar month in 278 BC.
NARRATOR 1:	He preferred death to the sadness he felt…
NARRATOR 2:	…because he could not save his country.

Scene 5—Remembering Chu Yuan

SETTING: A village on the Mi-Lo River some years later. Onstage are Narrator 1, Narrator 2, Villager 1, Villager 2, Villager 3, and Villager 4.

NARRATOR 1:	The Dragon Boat Festival began in 227 BC.

NARRATOR 2:	To remember the poet who loved his country.
VILLAGER 1:	The Mi-Lo River is beautiful today.
VILLAGER 2:	Remember that poet who died here?
VILLAGER 3:	Yes—Chu Yuan.
VILLAGER 4:	He wrote some beautiful poems.
VILLAGER 5:	All about our country.
VILLAGER 6:	Chu Yuan really loved our country.
VILLAGER 1:	So do I.
VILLAGER 2:	Me, too.
VILLAGER 3:	We should have a festival to honor Chu Yuan.
VILLAGER 4:	So he'll be remembered forever.
VILLAGER 1:	And so people will want to be like him.
VILLAGER 2:	I want to be like him.
VILLAGER 3:	Me, too.
VILLAGER 4:	And so people will want to serve our country.
VILLAGER 1:	I want to serve our country.
VILLAGER 2:	And be proud of it.
VILLAGER 3:	I'm proud of our country.
VILLAGER 4:	Me, too.
VILLAGER 1:	We could all ride boats.
VILLAGER 2:	Like the fishermen did.
VILLAGER 3:	When they tried to save Chu Yuan.
VILLAGER 4:	And we could pretend to search for Chu Yuan.
VILLAGER 1:	Let's decorate our boats.
VILLAGER 2:	We could carve dragons on our boats.
VILLAGER 3:	Good idea!
VILLAGER 4:	Dragons are powerful.
VILLAGER 1:	And they bring good luck.
VILLAGER 2:	Let's beat drums.
VILLAGER 3:	That will scare away the evil water spirits.
VILLAGER 4:	We could toss rice packets into the water…
VILLAGER 1:	…like the fishermen did.
VILLAGER 2:	So the fish wouldn't eat Chu Yuan's body.
VILLAGER 3:	But let's eat some of the rice, too!

VILLAGER 4:   And have a big party.

VILLAGER 1:   With food.

VILLAGER 2:   And fun.

VILLAGER 3:   We could race our dragon boats.

VILLAGER 4:   Each boat can be a team.

VILLAGER 1:   Chu Yuan would like that!

VILLAGER 2:   It would be a fun way for people to work together.

VILLAGER 3:   The dragons on the boats will protect our village.

VILLAGER 4:   This sounds like it will be fun.

VILLAGER 1:   So fun we should do it every year!

VILLAGER 2:   I like that idea!

VILLAGER 3:   Me, too!

VILLAGER 4:   So would Chu Yuan.

Scene 7—Epilogue

SETTING: Epilogue. Onstage are Narrator 1 and Narrator 2. The script has been separated at this point to allow additional readers to participate as new Narrators.

NARRATOR 1:   Every year the Chinese people honor Chu Yuan.

NARRATOR 2:   They celebrate his life.

NARRATOR 1:   They celebrate his poetry.

NARRATOR 2:   They celebrate his love for his country.

NARRATOR 1:   The Dragon Boat Festival became one of the most popular celebrations in China.

NARRATOR 2:   Today Dragon Boat races are held all over the world.

NARRATOR 1:   Emperor Chin united many small empires into one.

NARRATOR 2:   The country united by Emperor Chin is named after him.

NARRATOR 1:   It is called…

NARRATOR 1 and NARRATOR 2:   [in unison] Chin-a!

FOLLOW-UP ACTIVITIES

Where in the World Am I? (Geography)

Find China on a world map. Find the longitudinal and latitudinal boundaries of modern-day China. Locate the major rivers, mountains, and cities in China.

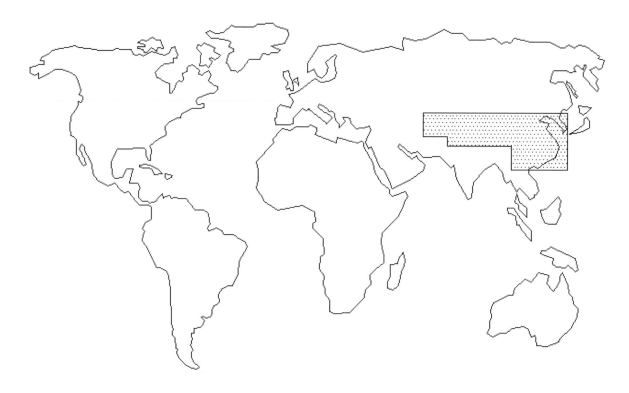

Make a Flag of China (Math, Art)

Today, the country that is China is called the Republic of China. Its form of government is communist. Its flag is red with one large yellow star in the upper left corner and 4 smaller yellow stars in an arc to the right of the large star. To make a flag of China, you will need:

- ❖ Sheet of 9-inch by 12-inch red construction paper
- ❖ ½ sheet of yellow paper
- ❖ Ruler
- ❖ Scissors
- ❖ Glue
- ❖ Pencil
- ❖ Large star pattern
- ❖ Small star pattern

Measure, mark, and cut the red paper to a size 8 inches by 12 inches. Photocopy the star patterns onto yellow paper, or make patterns and trace them onto yellow construction paper. Cut out.

Glue the large star onto the top left corner of the red paper. Glue the four smaller stars in an arc to the right of the large star as shown, so that one point of each of the smaller stars is pointing toward the center of the large star.

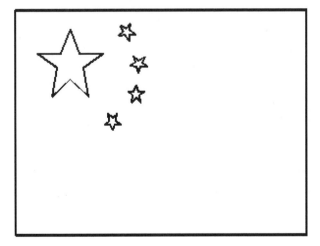

Discuss the colors and symbolism of the Chinese flag. Red is a traditional color of revolution—power achieved through bloodshed of the people. The large gold star represents the communist party. Each of the four small stars represents the four classes of citizens—workers, peasants, the middle class, and capitalists sympathetic to communism.

The ratio of the Chinese flag is 3:2 (length to width). Calculate the size of paper needed to double the size of the flag. Calculate the size of paper needed to make a flag half the size. Calculate or estimate the size of the stars needed for the larger- and smaller-size flags.

National Anthem of China (Literacy, Music)

The following are the lyrics to the national anthem of the Republic of China. Check the library or look online for a recording of the music.

Arise, ye who refuse to be slaves!
With our flesh and blood, let us build our new Great Wall!
The Chinese nation faces its greatest danger.
Everybody must roar his defiance.
Arise! Arise! Arise!
Millions with but one heart,
Braving the enemy's fire.
March on!
Braving the enemy's fire.
March on! March on! On!

Currency Conversion (Math)

Using an online currency converter or the financial section of a newspaper, look up the Chinese yuan. How does the value of a yuan compare to a US dollar? Calculate how many yuan it would cost to buy:

❖ A candy bar (at US $.50)

❖ A pizza (at US $10.00)

❖ A car (at US $15,000.00)

HAVE A DRAGON BOAT CELEBRATION

Snack on tea, rice balls drizzled with honey, and oranges or tangerines.

Rice Ball Recipe (Math)

The traditional food eaten at the Dragon Boat Festival is *zongzi* [pronounced ZONG-zee]. Zongzi is a rice dumpling tied in bamboo leaves and boiled. Sometimes dates, sweet red bean paste, or bits of pork are placed inside the rice for an extra treat. Zongzi are tricky to make because of the wrapping process, and because bamboo leaves are hard to find. You can substitute rice balls for zongzi in our Dragon Boat celebration. To make rice balls you will need:

❖ Hot plate and pan with lid, or electric rice cooker

❖ Large spoon

❖ Sticky rice (small-grained white rice) NOTE: long-grained or instant rice will not work for this recipe, because the rice must stick together. Follow the recipe on the rice package. One cup of uncooked sticky rice, made according to the package directions, will make approximately 20 rice balls of about 1 inch in diameter.

❖ Water—according to the directions for cooking rice

❖ Salt—according to the directions

❖ Measuring cup

❖ Measuring spoon

❖ Serving plate

❖ Napkins

Wash hands before cooking. Prepare the rice according to the directions, but without butter or oil. The finished rice balls will be small, so each student may want more than one.

When the rice has cooked, allow it to cool until it can be handled. Roll into balls and drizzle with honey just before serving. Eat with fingers or chopsticks! Rice balls can be made ahead of time at home and brought in to share with the class.

Traditional Zongzi Recipe (Science, Math)

The following is a traditional recipe for zongzi. It is probably too difficult to make in a classroom, but it can be read to begin a discussion about bamboo—where and how it is grown, what it looks like, and what it might taste like. The bamboo leaves used to wrap and cook the rice in are not eaten, but they give the rice a special flavor. To make traditional zongzi, you will need:

❖ 30 bamboo leaves

❖ Uncooked sticky rice (approximately 2 cups) soaked in water for 2 hours

❖ Chinese dried dates soaked in water for 12 hours

❖ Soft bristle brush

❖ Large pot

❖ Spoon for rice

❖ Cooking string

Drain the rice and the dates. Wash and scrub the bamboo leaves with a soft bristle brush. Take one bamboo leaf at a time and fold it flat at the stalk to make a "sheet." Using 2 or 3 bamboo leaf "sheets," overlap them in your hand until they form a funnel.

Place about ½ cup of uncooked sticky rice at the bottom of the bamboo funnel. Add several soaked dates and cover with another layer of rice. Fold the leaves over the open side of the funnel and tie the bundle with cooking string. Make sure the bundle is tight so it will not come loose during cooking.

Place the packets in a pot and cover them with water, making sure they are in the pot tightly so they do not bounce when boiled. Bring to a boil and then simmer for 2 hours on low. Makes 10 dumplings.

Dragon Head (Art)

To make dragon heads for the boats in Scene 7, or to decorate the classroom, you will need:

- ❖ Butcher paper—2 sheets for each dragon head
- ❖ Ruler
- ❖ Pencil
- ❖ Scissors
- ❖ Colored markers, crayons, paint (and brushes)
- ❖ Glue, yarn, colored paper, other items for decoration
- ❖ Newspapers

Measure the width of the back of a small chair that will be used as the front of a boat (a small student's classroom chair works well for this). Then measure and mark two sheets of butcher paper approximately 12 inches in height and the width of the chair back PLUS an additional 8 inches on all sides.

Place the two sheets of paper on top of each other and cut them together in an arc the size of the measurements, leaving one edge straight at the bottom of the "head."

Draw a face of a dragon on one of the sheets of paper. Add yarn, strips of colored paper, crinkled or spiraled pipe cleaners, glitter, buttons, or other decorations to the face.

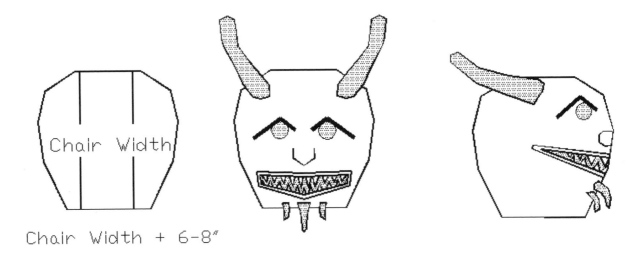

Staple the front and back of the head together along the curved sides, about 1 inch from the outside edge, leaving the bottom edge unstapled.

Lightly fill the inside of the head with crumpled newspapers and slip the head over the back of the chair, facing away from the seat. Attach additional ribbons, yarn, or crepe paper streamers as desired. The drummer can sit on the chair—the front of the dragon boat.

Xiangbao Pouches (Science, Art)

Xiangbao [pronounced zjang-BOW] are colorful cotton or silk pouches filled with dried flowers to ward off poisonous creatures. They are traditionally made and worn at Dragon Boat Festivals. Discuss the flower-drying process. To make xiangbao you will need:

❖ Colorful fabric

❖ Length of yarn approximately 36 inches long

❖ Dried potpourri—approximately 1 tablespoon for each xiangbao

❖ Scissors

Cut one 8-inch square of fabric for each xiangbao. Place 1 tablespoon of dried potpourri in the center of the fabric square. Fold the yarn in half so that it is a double length of 18 inches. Gather the edges of the fabric together and hold with one hand. With the other hand, tightly wind the yarn around the fabric several times, leaving approximately 1 inch of fabric edge above the yarn. Tie to secure the pouch, leaving the ends of the yarn loose so you can tie the xiangbao around your neck or attach it to your belt.

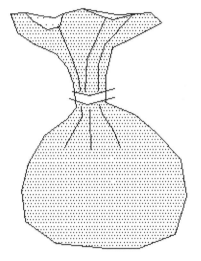

SUGGESTIONS FOR FURTHER ACTIVITIES

History: Research Emperor Chin and the unification of China.

History: Research the archaeology of Emperor Chin's tomb and his army of terra cotta warriors found guarding it.

Social Studies: Research Chinese customs and beliefs regarding dragons—what dragons represent, what powers they have, and dragons in Chinese art and literature.

History/Literacy: Research the life of Chu Yuan. Read some of his poems.

Language Arts: Have students write a poem about what they love about their country, city, or school.

Science: Discuss a lunar month and how it relates to a month of our calendar. (See the chapter entitled **Calendars.**)

Math: When making rice balls, discuss measurement conversions. Then practice converting fractions and whole numbers and ounces and metric system measurements, using the recipe as a guide. (See the chapter entitled **Measurements and Metric Conversions.**)

July—Independence Day

(United States)

BACKGROUND

July 4, 1776 marked the date when colonial America formally declared its independence from England. Thus began the Americans' long fight for freedom and self-government. Every year Americans celebrate the birth of our country on July 4—Independence Day.

READERS THEATRE SCRIPT—FREEDOM ISN'T FREE

Suggested Costumes and Props

- ❖ Empty boxes for tea chests (Scene 2)
- ❖ Papers (Scenes 6 and 7)
- ❖ Chair for Thomas Jefferson (Scene 6)

Characters

The following is a list of characters.

- NARRATOR 1
- NARRATOR 2
- TOWN CRIER
- COLONIST 1
- COLONIST 2
- COLONIST 3
- COLONIST 4
- BOSTON RAIDER 1
- BOSTON RAIDER 2
- BOSTON RAIDER 3
- BOSTON RAIDER 4
- CONGRESSPERSON 1
- CONGRESSPERSON 2
- CONGRESSPERSON 3
- CONGRESSPERSON 4
- THOMAS JEFFERSON
- JOHN ADAMS
- BENJAMIN FRANKLIN
- ROBERT R. LIVINGSTON
- ROGER SHERMAN
- BRITISH SOLDIERS, TOWNSPEOPLE, RAIDERS, AND CONGRESSPEOPLE (nonspeaking)

Presentation Suggestions

This play includes 7 scenes. Narrator 1 and Narrator 2 will be onstage at all times. Consider decorating the back of the stage with a large American flag, or with the flags made by students. The **SETTING** at the beginning of each scene is to assist the characters and is not intended to be read. Performance suggestions (gestures, movements, facial expressions) and pronunciation helps are included in brackets.

Freedom Isn't Free

Scene 1—The Stamp Tax

SETTING: Colonial America, 1765. Onstage are Narrator 1, Narrator 2, Town Crier, Colonists 1, 2, 3, and 4.

NARRATOR 1:	In 1763, England won a war it was fighting with France.
NARRATOR 2:	The war was called the French and Indian War.
NARRATOR 1:	It was fought in North America.
NARRATOR 2:	The year is now 1765.
NARRATOR 1:	England now controlled most of North America. . .
NARRATOR 2	. . . including the 13 colonies.
NARRATOR 1:	But the war cost England a lot of money.
NARRATOR 2:	To pay for the war, England taxed the colonies.
TOWN CRIER:	Big news!
COLONIST 1:	What now?
TOWN CRIER:	England has given us a new tax!
COLONIST 2:	Boo!
TOWN CRIER:	It's called the Stamp Act.
COLONIST 3:	What does that mean?
TOWN CRIER:	It means we have to pay a tax if we want to buy any paper.
COLONIST 4:	Oh, no! I use a lot of paper in my business.
COLONIST 1:	So do I.
COLONIST 2:	England keeps taxing us. . .
COLONIST 3:	. . .and we don't even have a say in how we're governed.
COLONIST 4:	That's taxation without representation!
COLONIST 1:	That's not fair!
COLONIST 1, 2, 3, and 4:	[chanting in unison] No fair! No fair! No fair!

From *Around the World Through Holidays: Cross Curricular Readers Theatre* written and illustrated by Carol Peterson. Westport, CT: Teacher Ideas Press/Libraries Unlimited. Copyright © 2006.

Scene 2—The Boston Messes

SETTING: Colonial America. Onstage are Narrator 1, Narrator 2, several nonspeaking colonists, and British soldiers. Later onstage are Boston Raider 1, Boston Raider 2, Boston Raider 3, and Boston Raider 4.

NARRATOR 1: England continued to tax the colonies to pay for the war.

NARRATOR 2: England thought the colonies should help pay for the colonies' defense.

NARRATOR 1: But the colonists didn't think it was fair to be taxed and not be represented in government.

NARRATOR 1: Many colonists formed groups to protest the taxes.

NARRATOR 2: A group in Boston even threatened British tax collectors.

NARRATOR 1: So England placed soldiers in Boston…

NARRATOR 2: …to protect the tax collectors.

NARRATOR 1: During a 1770 tax protest, British troops fired at the protestors.

NARRATOR 2: The soldiers killed 5 colonial protesters.

[Nonspeaking colonists and British soldiers enter from stage left or stage right. Colonists shake their fists at the soldiers; soldiers fire on the colonists. Five colonists fall down.]

NARRATOR 1: This first blood of the revolution had been spilled.

NARRATOR 2: The event was called the "Boston Massacre."

NARRATOR 1: What is a "massacre?

NARRATOR 2: A massacre is the killing of helpless people.

NARRATOR 1: Wow. And then England continued to tax the colonists.

NARRATOR 2: Tea was another item that was taxed.

NARRATOR 1: Many colonists came to America from England.

NARRATOR 2: They really loved drinking tea.

NARRATOR 1: But they didn't like having to pay a big tax on it.

NARRATOR 2: Then England told one tea company it could sell all of the tea in the colonies.

NARRATOR 1: The colonists didn't like that idea.

NARRATOR 2: So one night the colonists came up with a plan.

[Boston Raiders sneak onstage from stage left or stage right]

BOSTON RAIDER 1:	Hey, you look good dressed like a Mohawk!
BOSTON RAIDER 2:	Be quiet. Don't let anyone hear us.
BOSTON RAIDER 3:	What's the plan?
BOSTON RAIDER 4:	We sneak on board the ship.
BOSTON RAIDER 1:	Which ship?
BOSTON RAIDER 2:	The one owned by the East India Company.
BOSTON RAIDER 3:	The one bringing tea to sell here in the colonies.
BOSTON RAIDER 4:	And then what?
BOSTON RAIDER 1:	We find the barrels of tea.
BOSTON RAIDER 2:	And throw them overboard.
BOSTON RAIDER 3:	Throw them overboard?
BOSTON RAIDER 4:	Won't that mean no tea for us?
BOSTON RAIDER 1:	Yes, but it also means no money for the tea company.
BOSTON RAIDER 2:	And no tax for England!
BOSTON RAIDER 3:	Maybe the King will see that we mean business!
BOSTON RAIDER 4:	He can't keep taxing the colonies to pay for his war.
BOSTON RAIDER 1:	Without letting us be represented in government.
BOSTON RAIDER 2:	No taxation without representation!
BOSTON RAIDER 3:	Everybody ready?
BOSTON RAIDER 4:	Let's go!

[Boston Raiders grab boxes and throw them "overboard"]

Scene 3—The Intolerable Acts

SETTING: Later. Onstage are Narrator 1, Narrator 2, Town Crier, Colonist 1, Colonist 2, Colonist 3, and Colonist 4.

NARRATOR 1:	The protestors at the Boston Tea Party threw 342 chests of tea into Boston Harbor.
NARRATOR 2:	Three hundred forty-two chests of tea?
NARRATOR 1:	Yes.
NARRATOR 2:	That's a lot of tea!
NARRATOR 1:	England wasn't happy.
NARRATOR 2:	As a result, England made more laws.

TOWN CRIER:	Listen everyone! New laws.
COLONIST 1:	Now what?
TOWN CRIER:	Boston Harbor is closed.
COLONIST 2:	What? That's intolerable!
TOWN CRIER:	And protestors who are caught will be sent back to England for trial.
COLONIST 3:	Sent all the way back to England for trial?
TOWN CRIER:	Yes.
COLONIST 4:	That's intolerable!
TOWN CRIER:	And we must let British soldiers stay in our homes.
COLONIST 1:	British soldiers in our homes?
COLONIST 2:	I'm not going to let soldiers take over my house!
COLONIST 3:	Me neither!
COLONIST 4:	That's intolerable!
NARRATOR 1:	Colonists called these new laws and two others the Intolerable Acts.
NARRATOR 2:	The laws made the colonists even angrier.

Scene 4—The First Continental Congress

SETTING: Colonial America, 1774. Onstage are Narrator 1, Narrator 2, Congressperson 1, Congressperson 2, Congressperson 3, and Congressperson 4.

NARRATOR 1:	The year is 1774.
NARRATOR 2:	Twelve of the thirteen colonies sent representatives to Philadelphia. . .
NARRATOR 1:	. . . for the First Continental Congress to decide what to do about England.
NARRATOR 2:	Georgia didn't send a representative, but agreed to support the Congress's plans.
NARRATOR 1:	Let's see what that meeting might have been like.
CONGRESSPERSON 1:	Okay, everyone settle down.
CONGRESSPERSON 2:	How we can improve our relationship with England?
CONGRESSPERSON 3:	We can't!
CONGRESSPERSON 1:	We need to try.

CONGRESSPERSON 4:   Yes, after all, we're Englishmen, too.

CONGRESSPERSON 3:   Not anymore.

CONGRESSPERSON 4:   Right! England has gone too far!

NARRATOR 1:   The Congress was held to try to restore relations with England.

NARRATOR 2:   But in the end, the representatives decided it was too late.

NARRATOR 1:   Instead, they declared taxation and the Intolerable Acts "unconstitutional."

NARRATOR 2:   They decided not to pay taxes, and they told colonists to arm themselves.

Scene 5—War Begins

SETTING: Lexington, Virginia, on April 19, 1775. Onstage are Narrator 1, Narrator 2, Colonist 1, Colonist 2, and several British soldiers.

NARRATOR 1:   Things were bad between the colonists and the British soldiers.

NARRATOR 2:   Finally on April 19, 1775, in Lexington, Virginia, something happened that started war.

COLONIST 1:   Hey! Those British soldiers are trying to take over the building where we keep our guns.

COLONIST 2:   Stop them!

[British soldiers march across the stage]

[Sound of gunfire offstage]

[A British soldier falls down]

COLONIST 1:   Did you hear that shot?

COLONIST 2:   I'll bet that shot was heard around the world!

NARRATOR 1:   The shot at Lexington, Virginia became famous.

NARRATOR 2:   It was called "the shot heard round the world."

NARRATOR 1:   Not because the sound was loud.

NARRATOR 2:   But because it was an important event in history.

NARRATOR 1:   Eight colonists and 273 British soldiers were killed that day.

NARRATOR 2:   The Revolutionary War had begun.

Scene 6—Second Continental Congress

SETTING: Philadelphia, Pennsylvania, on May 10, 1775—the Second Continental Congress. Present onstage are Narrator 1, Narrator 2, Congressperson 1, Congressperson 2, Congressperson 3, Congressperson 4, Thomas Jefferson, John Adams, Benjamin Franklin, Roger Sherman, and Robert R. Livingston.

NARRATOR 1: On May 10, 1775, the Second Continental Congress met…

NARRATOR 2: …in Philadelphia, Pennsylvania.

CONGRESSPERSON 1: Okay—this is it! WE are now the government in the colonies.

CONGRESSPERSON 2: Yeah! We've got a government and an army.

CONGRESSPERSON 3: I nominate George Washington to be in charge of the army.

CONGRESSPERSON 4: Who's in favor of George Washington as Commander in Chief?

[All the Congresspeople raise their hands and cheer]

CONGRESSPERSON 1: Okay, George Washington is in charge of the colonial army.

CONGRESSPERSON 2: So now we need to declare our independence from England.

CONGRESSPERSON 3: How do we do that?

CONGRESSPERSON 4: We should have an official statement.

CONGRESSPERSON 1: Something we could all sign.

CONGRESSPERSON 2: For the whole world to see.

CONGRESSPERSON 3: Who's willing to write up a Declaration of Independence?

CONGRESSPERSON 4: Thomas Jefferson would do a great job.

CONGRESSPERSON 1: We need a few people to help him.

[John Adams, Benjamin Franklin, Roger Sherman, and Robert R. Livingston raise their hands]

CONGRESSPERSON 2: John Adams, Benjamin Franklin, Roger Sherman, and Robert R. Livingston have volunteered.

[Everyone except Narrator 1, Narrator 2, Thomas Jefferson, John Adams, Benjamin Franklin, Roger Sherman, and Robert R. Livingston exit]

[Thomas Jefferson sits down and pretends to write]

NARRATOR 1: In June, 1776, Thomas Jefferson began writing a document…

NARRATOR 2:	…to declare that the colonies were now an independent nation.
JOHN ADAMS:	How's the writing coming, Tom?
THOMAS JEFFERSON:	I've got the first draft done.
JOHN ADAMS:	[looking over Thomas Jefferson's shoulder] You've been working really hard.
BENJAMIN FRANKLIN:	[points to the sky as if saying something important] There are no gains without pains.
THOMAS JEFFERSON:	Thanks for the wisdom, Ben.
ROGER SHERMAN:	Why does it say, "it becomes necessary"?
THOMAS JEFFERSON:	If we are going to form a new nation, the rest of the world will want to know why.
BENJAMIN FRANKLIN:	[points to the sky as if saying something important] Love your neighbor, but don't pull down your hedge.
ROBERT R. LIVINGSTON:	Great advice, Ben.
THOMAS JEFFERSON:	So we need to tell the world we had no other choice.
ROGER SHERMAN:	Because England was so unfair.
ROBERT R. LIVINGSTON:	But what does it mean, "separate and equal station"?
THOMAS JEFFERSON:	Our new nation deserves the same respect and authority as any other nation.
ROGER SHERMAN:	Right!
ROBERT R. LIVINGSTON:	Yes!
JOHN ADAMS:	That's for sure!
BENJAMIN FRANKLIN:	[points to the sky as if saying something important] Think of three things: Whence you came, where you are going, and to whom you must account.
THOMAS JEFFERSON:	Very helpful, Ben.
BENJAMIN FRANKLIN:	[points to the sky as if saying something important] And remember: Fish and visitors stink in three days.
JOHN ADAMS:	Lovely words of wisdom, Ben, but maybe you should go fly a kite.
BENJAMIN FRANKLIN:	Already did that. Okay. Let's get back to work. Because [points to the sky as if saying something important] laws too gentle are seldom obeyed; too severe, seldom executed.
THOMAS JEFFERSON:	Ah!
ROBERT R. LIVINGSTON:	Right!
JOHN ADAMS:	Good one, Ben!
ROGER SHERMAN:	That's the ticket!

Scene 7—More Declarations

SETTING: 1776—the Continental Congress meets again. Present onstage are Narrator 1, Narrator 2, Congressperson 1, Congressperson 2, Congressperson 3, Congressperson 4, and other Congresspersons.

NARRATOR 1:	The men worked on the Declaration of Independence all month.
NARRATOR 2:	On June 28, 1776, they presented it to the Congress.
CONGRESSPERSON 1:	Pretty good.
CONGRESSPERSON 2:	But we might change a few of the words.
NARRATOR 1:	After some more work on the Declaration. . .
NARRATOR 2:	. . .Congress met again on July 2, 1776.
CONGRESSPERSON 3:	Let's vote on whether we should declare our colonies an independent nation.
CONGRESSPERSON 4:	All in favor…
	[Congresspersons raise their hands and cheer]
NARRATOR 1:	And still congress continued to revise the Declaration.
NARRATOR 2:	Another 39 times.
NARRATOR 1:	What? Thirty-nine more revisions?
NARRATOR 2:	Yes—39 more revisions.
NARRATOR 1:	British troops landed in New York on July 2, 1776.
NARRATOR 2:	Finally, on the morning of July 4, 1776, Congress adopted the final version of the Declaration of Independence.
NARRATOR 1:	The Declaration was printed, published, and read.
	[Here the Narrators or other students can read part or all of the Declaration of Independence]
NARRATOR2:	A new nation had been formed.
NARRATOR 1:	The fight for America's freedom had begun.
NARRATOR 2:	America would soon learn…
NARRATORS 1 and 2:	…freedom isn't free.

The Declaration of Independence (Literacy)

The Declaration of Independence can be read during the play or as a separate activity. Here are its famous first two sentences:

> When in the Course of human events, it becomes necessary for one people to dissolve the political bands which have connected them with another, and to assume among the powers of the earth, the separate and equal station to which the laws of Nature and of Nature's God entitle them, a decent respect to the opinions of mankind requires that they should declare the causes which impel them to the separation.
>
> We hold these truths to be self-evident, that all men are created equal, that they are endowed by their Creator with certain unalienable Rights, that among these are Life, Liberty and the pursuit of Happiness.

FOLLOW-UP ACTIVITIES

Where in the World Am I? (Geography)

Find the United States of America on a world map. Locate the major rivers and mountains and the longitudinal and latitudinal boundaries. Locate each of the 50 state capitals.

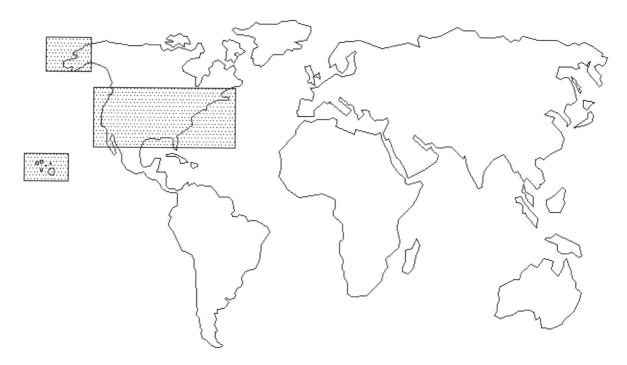

Make a Flag of Colonial America (Math, Art)

The first Flag Act passed by the Continental Congress on June 14, 1777, says: "Resolved, that the flag of the United States be made of thirteen stripes, alternate red and white; that the union be thirteen stars, white in a blue field, representing a new Constellation." The colonial flag here has stars placed in a circle so that no one colony would be higher up. The official ratio of the American flag is 10:19. Because we are using standard-size construction paper for our flag, the ratios will be approximate. To make a colonial flag you will need:

- ❖ Sheet of white construction paper, 9 inches by 12 inches
- ❖ Blue construction paper
- ❖ Red construction paper
- ❖ Reproducible stars copied onto white paper
- ❖ Scissors
- ❖ Ruler
- ❖ Pencil
- ❖ Compass
- ❖ Glue

Using the ruler, pencil, and scissors, measure, mark, and cut a sheet of blue paper into a 4¾-inch square. Then measure, mark, and cut 7 strips of red paper ¾ inches wide by 12 inches long. NOTE: The construction paper can be cut ahead of time using a paper cutter, but allowing students to measure the paper creates an additional math tie-in. To save paper, have students work in pairs—one measuring and cutting the blue paper; one measuring and cutting the red paper.

Place the white paper in front of you horizontally. Glue one of the ¾-inch by 12-inch red strips at the top edge of the white paper, matching edges. Glue a second red strip at the bottom edge of the white paper, matching edges. Using your ruler as a guide, glue the remaining 5 red strips of paper onto the white paper, leaving inch of white showing between each red strip. Then glue the blue square onto the upper left edge, over the red and white stripes and matching top and left edges.

Using a compass and pencil, draw a circle in the middle of the blue square with a diameter of approximately 3½ inches. Cut out the 13 stars and glue them equidistantly around the circle. Erase the penciled circle.

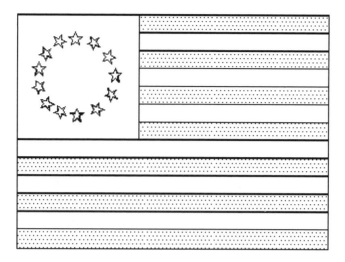

Introduce and compute the diameter, circumference, and area of the circle used for this flag. Discuss different types of stars, including the number of points. Break a star shape down geometrically into triangles and discuss how altering the angles would change the shape of stars, and how adding points would change the angle of the points. Discuss the flag's ratio of 10:19. What would a flag measure at half size and at double size, using the same ratio?

National Anthem of the United States (Literacy, History, Music)

Less than 35 years after America won independence, it declared war on England because of trading arguments America had with England while England was fighting a new war with France. England then attacked the United States, burning down the White House, the Capitol Building, and the Library of Congress in Washington, DC. England then tried to capture nearby Baltimore, Maryland.

America prepared for the British invasion of Fort McHenry in Baltimore. The fort commander had a special flag made. The 30- by 42-foot flag was so big the British fleet would be able to see it from the harbor. On September 13, 1814, the British began firing bombs and rockets at Fort McHenry. The bombing lasted for 25 hours. A young lawyer, Francis Scott Key, watched in the early morning darkness the next day to see if the huge flag was still flying over the fort. If the flag was still flying, it would mean the Americans had not lost. When Mr. Key saw the flag in the dawn light, he was inspired to write the words to a song. Congress made it our national anthem in 1931.

Here are the lyrics to the first verse. Sing and/or read aloud and discuss.

Oh say can you see
By the dawn's early light
What so proudly we hailed
At the twilight's last gleaming?
Whose broad stripes and bright stars,
Through the perilous fight,
O'er the ramparts we watched
Were so gallantly streaming?

And the rockets' red glare,
The bombs bursting in air,
Gave proof through the night
That our flag was still there.
Oh say does that star-spangled
Banner yet wave
O'er the land of the free
And the home of the brave?

Currency Conversion (Math)

The colonies formerly belonged to England. The currency used in England is the pound. Using an online currency converter or the financial section of a newspaper look up the British pound. How does the value of a pound compare with a US dollar? Imagine what it would be like if America still used the currency of England, and calculate how many pounds it would cost to buy:

❖ A candy bar (at US $.50)

❖ A pizza (at US $10.00)

❖ A car (at US $15,000.00)

HAVE AN INDEPENDENCE DAY CELEBRATION

Snack on tea and johnnycakes. Drink your tea as the English colonists might have—hot, with sugar and cream. Johnnycakes can be made as a classroom activity.

Johnnycakes Recipe (Math)

Johnnycakes were a popular food in early America. They were often cooked on a black iron pan in the fireplace and eaten for breakfast. Sometimes they were eaten with apple butter or maple syrup. To make 12 cakes, you will need:

❖ 1 cup hot water

❖ 2 tablespoons oil

❖ 1 cup yellow cornmeal

❖ ½ teaspoon salt

❖ 1 tablespoon sugar

❖ ½ cup milk

❖ Shortening or oil to grease the frying pan

❖ Optional apple butter or maple syrup

❖ Measuring cup

❖ Measuring spoons

❖ Mixing bowl

❖ Wooden spoon

❖ Electric frying pan

❖ Spatula for turning johnnycakes

❖ Paper plates, forks, and napkins

Wash hands before cooking. Mix dry ingredients in the bowl. Add hot water, oil, and milk. Stir with wooden spoon until batter is mixed. Heat a small amount of oil or shortening in electric frying pan, on medium heat.

Drop 3 or 4 spoonfuls of batter into the hot frying pan and cook until bubbles appear on the surface of the johnnycakes (about 3 to 4 minutes). Using the spatula, flip the johnnycakes over and cook on the other side. Remove the cooked johnnycakes from the pan with the spatula, and serve. Serve with apple butter or maple syrup.

Discuss and calculate new measurements to double or triple this recipe. Recalculate measurements from standard to metric measurements. See the chapter entitled **Measurements and Metric Conversions.**

Learn the Names of the Thirteen Colonies (Literacy, History)

These are the names of the original thirteen colonies and the order in which they ratified the new Constitution.

1 Delaware	2 Pennsylvania
3 New Jersey	4 Georgia
5 Connecticut	6 Massachusetts
7 Maryland	8 South Carolina
9 New Hampshire	10 Virginia
11 New York	12 North Carolina
13 Rhode Island	

Have students read the following story to decipher the names of the colonies. Although Del can't spell, memorizing this story will help students remember the order in which the thirteen colonies joined the union.

Poor Del Can't Spell. DEL had no paper, so he took his PEN and wrote a letter on his NEW football JERSEY.

Dear GEORGIA,

I had to CONNECT a MASS of stuff for MARY, SO CAROLINA could help carry the NEW HAM she bought. It's VIRY far to NEW YORK and I have NO CAR. So we RHODE to Long ISLAND on our bikes.

Dominoes (Math)

Dominoes have been played for thousands of years. They became popular in the 1700s throughout Europe and came to the American colonies with the settlers. Here is one of the many different games that can be played with dominoes. A set of store-bought dominoes can be used, or students can make their own set, using precut rectangles of heavy card stock.

To make a set of dominoes with all number combinations from the doublet 0–0 through the doublet 6–6, you will need a felt pen and 28 rectangles approximately 1 inch by 2 inches. Draw a line horizontally across the middle of each domino tile to create halves for two sets of numbered dots. Create a set of 28 tiles to include the following number patterns—one on each side of the halfway line.

0-0
0-1
0-2
0-3 through 0-6
1-1
1-2
1-3 through 1-6
2-2
2-3
2-4 through 2-6

Continue with doublets 3-3 through doublet 6-6

The following dot patterns are used to show numbers 1 through 6. The tile is left blank to show the number zero.

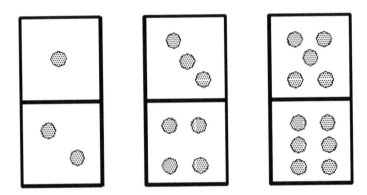

Discuss the math involved in the number of tiles needed to show all combinations from 0–0 to 6–6.

Groups of 2 to 4 students can play a game of dominoes called Draw. All domino tiles are placed face down in the middle of the table. Each player draws three dominoes from the pile and looks at them, but keeps them secret from the other players. Leave the remaining dominoes face down in the center. The extra dominoes are called the *bone yard*.

The person who has the doublet with the highest number (the 6–6) goes first by laying that domino in the center of the table, face up. If no one has the 6–6 doublet, the player with the next-highest-number doublet plays first (5–5, or 4–4, and so on). The player on the first player's right then lays down a domino with a matching number of dots against the doublet. Doublets are laid sideways and other dominoes are laid end-to-end, as shown.

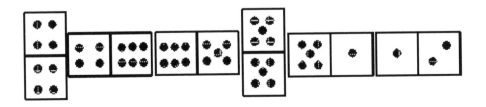

If the second player cannot match the number, he must take a tile from the bone yard until he finds a match. The next player must lay down a match at the free end of either the doublet or the second tile, taking a new tile from the bone yard if necessary. Play continues, matching the number of dots on the tiles and taking new tiles from the bone yard as needed. The first person to lay down all of his tiles is the winner.

Go Fly a Kite! (Math, Science, Art)

Benjamin Franklin was an inventor. One of the things he was interested in was electricity. One famous experiment he performed was to fly a kite during an electrical storm to understand what would happen if metal (a key he had attached to the kite) were struck by the electricity from lightning. As a result of his experiments, Benjamin Franklin is credited with a number of inventions. One invention was the lightning rod—a metal pole attached to the roof of a building. If lightning should strike the building, the rod would "catch" the electricity and prevent it from harming people inside the building.

To celebrate Benjamin Franklin's famous experiments, students make and fly simple sled kites. Research electrical storms, electricity, wind, or lift. To make a sled kite, you will need:

- ❖ 2 large paper grocery bags (1 for the wings, 1 for the body)
- ❖ Scissors
- ❖ Masking tape
- ❖ Hole punch or nail
- ❖ Roll of string

Cut open the paper bags, remove the bottoms, and lay the bags out flat. Cut wings from one of the bags as shown. Tape wings to the second flattened grocery bag. Place a piece of tape on the corner of each wing to strengthen the paper where shown. Then punch a hole through both the tape and the wing. Tie a length of string about 12 inches long through each hole. Cut a vent at the bottom of the kite to allow air to blow through it. Tie the ends of the two 12-inch strings together and attach them to a roll of string.

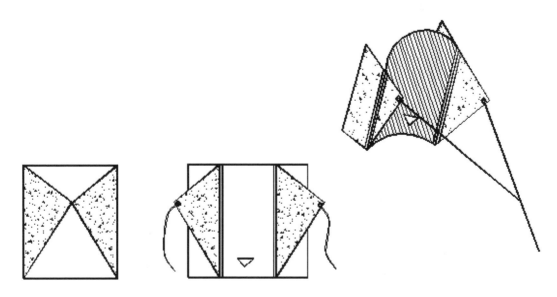

Before flying kites, review and discuss safety rules:

❖ Fly kites only in good weather.

❖ Never use metal on your kite that might attract lightning.

❖ Fly kites in an open field.

❖ Stay away from electrical wires.

❖ If your kite gets caught in a wire or tree, ask an adult if it can be removed safely.

SUGGESTIONS FOR FURTHER ACTIVITIES

History: Research the life of one or more of the signers of the Declaration of Independence.

Social Studies/Geography: Locate the original 13 colonies on a map. Then use a map without the state names listed (cover the state names and photocopy the map) and have students name the states by their shape.

Literacy: Many of Benjamin Franklin's lines in the script came from his publication, *Poor Richard's Almanac*. Find a copy of *Poor Richard's Almanac* and read some of the wisdom and wit of Benjamin Franklin.

Literacy: Read and discuss the poem, "Paul Revere's Ride," by Henry Wadsworth Longfellow.

Science: Research tea. Locate where it grows in the world, what the plant looks like, and what type of climate it needs.

Science: Maple syrup was used frequently as a sweetener and for seasoning foods in colonial North America. Research maple trees and how syrup is gathered and made.

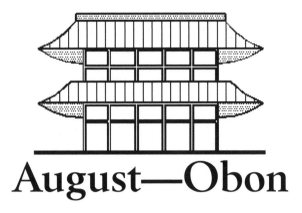

August—Obon

(Japan)

BACKGROUND

The Obon [pronounced OH-bon] festival is celebrated in Japan by people of both the Buddhist and the Shinto religions. They believe that ancestors' spirits return to this world to visit relatives during Obon. Obon is celebrated from July 13 through15 or from August 13 through 15, depending on whether the solar or the lunar calendar is used. (See the chapter entitled **Calendars**.)

READERS THEATRE SCRIPT—UNTIL NEXT YEAR, GRANDPA SATO

Suggested Costumes and Props

- ❖ Pillows and blankets (Scene 1)
- ❖ Large grocery bag (Scene 2)
- ❖ Bowls, pans (Scene 3)
- ❖ Drums (boxes or barrels) and sticks (Scene 5)
- ❖ Paper fans (Scene 5)
- ❖ Paper lanterns (Scenes 3 and 4)
- ❖ Brooms, rags, bucket (Scene 4)
- ❖ Cut branches or artificial plants (Scene 4)

Characters

The following is a list of characters. Nonspeaking roles include neighbors and dancers.

- NARRATOR 1
- NARRATOR 2
- MOTHER SATO
- FATHER SATO
- GRANDMOTHER SATO

- HARU
- UMEKO
- MR. YAMADA
- NEIGHBORS (nonspeaking)
- DANCERS (nonspeaking)

Presentation Suggestions

This play includes 5 scenes. Narrator 1 and Narrator 2 will be onstage at all times. Consider decorating the back of the stage with a backdrop, made from butcher paper, that depicts a landscape and a river or lake, or with individual Japanese flags made by students. The **SETTING** at the beginning of each scene is to assist the characters and is not intended to be read. Performance suggestions (gestures, movements, facial expressions) and pronunciation helps are included in brackets.

Until Next Year, Grandpa Sato

Scene 1— The First Day of Obon

SETTING: Summertime in Japan at the home of the Sato family. Onstage are Narrator 1, Narrator 2, Umeko, her brother Haru, Mother and Father Sato. Umeko and Haru are sleeping.

NARRATOR 1:	It is summer in Japan.
NARRATOR 2:	Time for the Obon festival.
MOTHER:	Good morning, children.
UMEKO:	It's so early!
HARU:	May I sleep some more?
FATHER:	No, it's time to get up.
MOTHER:	It's a special day.
UMEKO:	What special day?
FATHER:	It's August 13.
MOTHER:	The first day of Obon!
HARU and UMEKO:	[getting out of bed] Obon!
FATHER:	Get dressed, Haru, and we'll go to the lantern maker's shop.
UMEKA:	Is Grandmother Sato coming today?
MOTHER:	Yes, she is bringing something special.
FATHER:	I have set a mat before our home altar.
MOTHER:	Good! We'll place oranges and flowers there to remember Grandfather Sato.
HARU:	I miss Grandfather Sato.
UMEKO:	I'm so sad that he died.
HARU:	Grandfather Sato used to love oranges.

From *Around the World Through Holidays: Cross Curricular Readers Theatre* written and illustrated by Carol Peterson. Westport, CT: Teacher Ideas Press/Libraries Unlimited. Copyright © 2006.

FATHER: Yes, he would be happy we are putting oranges on our altar in his honor.

MOTHER: Get dressed, Umeko, and you can help me fix the picnic lunch.

HARU and UMEKO: We love Obon!

Scene 2—The Lantern Shop

SETTING: Later that day, at the shop that sells paper lanterns. Onstage are Narrator 1, Narrator 2, Father Sato, Haru, and the shop owner, Mr. Yamada.

NARRATOR 1: Father Sato and Haru arrive at the lantern shop.

NARRATOR 2: There are many types and colors of paper lanterns.

FATHER: Hello, Mr. Yamada.

MR. YAMADA: Hello, Mr. Sato.

FATHER: We've come to buy Obon lanterns.

MR. YAMADA: What do you need?

HARU: Let's get that big red one.

FATHER: And a green one.

HARU: And a blue one, too.

FATHER: We also need one for grandfather.

HARU: Yes, one for grandfather.

FATHER: Grandfather Sato died last September.

MR. YAMADA: He died after the last Obon festival?

FATHER: Yes.

MR. YAMADA: Then you'll need a white one for him.

HARU: We'll need some floating lanterns, too.

FATHER: Yes, let's get five of them.

MR. YAMADA: I have everything you need.

FATHER: Thank you. Here is the money.

HARU: See you later, Mr. Yamada!

Scene 3—At Home

SETTING: Later that day at the Sato home. Onstage are Narrator 1, Narrator 2, Umeko, Mother Sato, and Grandmother Sato. Later onstage are Haru and Father Sato.

NARRATOR 1:	At home, Umeko and her mother are preparing food.
NARRATOR 2:	Umeko's grandmother arrives.
UMEKO:	Hello, Grandmother Sato.
GRANDMOTHER SATO:	Hello, Umeko. I brought a nice cake.
UMEKO:	Yum! It looks wonderful.
MOTHER:	I've made the rice.
UMEKO:	I'll help you cut vegetables, Mother.
MOTHER:	And we'll have fruit, too.
UMEKO:	Mother said you were bringing something special, Grandmother.
GRANDMOTHER SATO:	Yes, I brought a little cage. Do you see our friend inside?
UMEKO:	A cricket! Oh, he sounds so happy.
MOTHER:	He will make our house cheerful.
UMEKO:	When do we leave for the cemetery?
MOTHER:	As soon as Father and Haru return with the lanterns.
	[Father and Haru enter]
FATHER:	We're home.
HARU:	And we have all the lanterns we need.
MOTHER:	We have the altar prepared.
GRANDMOTHER SATO:	And the picnic lunch is ready.
FATHER:	Haru and Umeko, get a broom and some rags and let's go.

Scene 4—The Cemetery

SETTING: Later that day at the cemetery. Onstage are Narrator 1, Narrator 2, Haru, Umeko, Father Sato, Mother Sato, and Grandmother Sato. Additional nonspeaking neighbors may also be present.

NARRATOR 1: The family arrived at the cemetery.

NARRATOR 2: Other families are there, too.

FATHER: Haru, help me sweep off the graves.

MOTHER: Let's pick these weeds.

GRANDMOTHER SATO: And wash off the gravestones.

NARRATOR 1: Haru and Father sweep.

NARRATOR 2: Umeko, mother, and grandmother pick weeds and wipe off the gravestones.

UMEKO: Let's find some flowers and green branches to decorate Grandfather Sato's grave.

GRANDMOTHER SATO: I miss Grandfather. I can't believe he died almost a year ago.

FATHER: We all miss him.

MOTHER: But at least his spirit can return home during Obon.

UMEKO: Let's eat our picnic lunch.

HARU: Don't forget to set out some food for Grandfather Sato's spirit.

NARRATOR 1: The family enjoys a picnic lunch.

NARRATOR 2: They talk about their loved ones who have died.

GRANDMOTHER SATO: Grandfather Sato's grave looks nice. He will be happy we care.

FATHER: [waving] Look—there are our neighbors.

HARU: [waving] Hello, Mrs. Tanaka.

UMEKO: [waving] Hello, Mr. Watanabe.

MOTHER: I'm sure they're remembering their ancestors, too.

FATHER: It is beginning to get dark.

HARU: Shall we light our lanterns?

MOTHER: Yes, and then we'll return home.

FATHER: And the spirits will follow us home.

UMEKO:	How will the spirits find their way to our house in the dark?
GRANDMOTHER SATO:	The lanterns will light the way for the spirits, just as they light our way.
UMEKO:	What about Grandfather's spirit? His spirit has never been part of Obon before.
HARU:	Umeko, you see the big, white lantern?
UMEKO:	Yes, here it is.
HARU:	That one is special to light the way for Grandfather's spirit.
UMEKO:	That's good. Grandfather will surely find his way home.
NARRATOR 1:	The families light their lanterns and carry them home.
NARRATOR 2:	And the spirits follow.

Scene 5—Bon Odori

SETTING: The center of town, three days later. Onstage are Narrator 1, Narrator 2, Haru, Umeko, Father Sato, Mother Sato, Grandmother Sato, and additional nonspeaking neighbors.

NARRATOR 1:	The spirits have followed their loved ones home.
NARRATOR 2:	And have spent three days on earth.
NARRATOR 1:	The people then celebrate with a dance.
NARRATOR 2:	The dance is called the **bon odori**.
	[pronounced bone oh-DOH-ree]
NARRATOR 1:	The people believe the dancing and music comfort the dead spirits.
MOTHER:	It's time for the bon odori!
UMEKO:	My favorite part of Obon. Are you coming, Haru?
FATHER:	Haru has a special part in the bon odori this year.
HARU:	I'm helping Father.
UMEKO:	This will be the best bon odori ever!
NARRATOR 1:	Haru and Father walk to the center of the circle of dancers.
NARRATOR 2:	There Haru and Father find special drums.
NARRATOR 1:	The Japanese word for drum is **taiko**.

[pronounced TAI-ko]

NARRATOR 2: These drums are two-sided.

NARRATOR 1: Haru and Father begin to beat the drums.

NARRATOR 2: The dance begins.

[Umeko, Mother Sato, Grandmother Sato, and other characters walk in a circle while Haru and Father beat drums at the center of the circle.]

Scene 6—Toro Nagashi

SETTING: Near the river, at the end of the Obon festival. Onstage are Narrator 1, Narrator 2, Haru, Umeko, Father Sato, Mother Sato, Grandmother Sato, and additional nonspeaking neighbors.

NARRATOR 1: It is the end of the Obon festival.

NARRATOR 2: Time for the spirits to leave this world.

[Haru, Umeko, Father Sato, Mother Sato, and Grandmother Sato walk across the stage and back]

UMEKO: How far until we reach the river?

FATHER: We're almost there.

UMEKO: Has the Toro Nagashi started yet?

[pronounced TOW-row nah-GASH-ee]

HARU: I can see the river now.

FATHER: No one has started floating lanterns yet.

MOTHER: Do you have your lanterns, everyone?

HARU: Yes, I have one.

UMEKO: I have one, too.

GRANDMOTHER SATO: I wrote Grandfather's name on my lantern.

HARU and UMEKO: So did we.

MOTHER: We must light our lanterns.

FATHER: So the spirits will see their way.

NARRATOR 1: The Toro Nagashi ceremony is the last part of the Obon festival.

NARRATOR 2:	It is when tiny lanterns are floated on the ocean, lake, or river.
FATHER:	There is a nice breeze tonight.
MOTHER:	The breeze will carry our lanterns out to sea.
GRANDMOTHER SATO:	Where the spirits can return to heaven.
UMEKO:	Light my lantern please, Father.
HARU:	Light mine, too, please.
NARRATOR 1:	Father lights everyone's lanterns.
NARRATOR 2:	The family thinks about their dead loved ones.
NARRATOR 1:	Then they place the lanterns on the water.
NARRATOR 2:	And watch the lanterns float away.
HARU:	Look at the patterns of light the little lanterns make.
UMEKO:	It's beautiful.
FATHER:	Just think of the love and memories all these lanterns represent.
MOTHER:	It's nice to remember people we love.
HARU:	Good-bye, Grandfather Sato.
UMEKO:	Come back again next year.
EVERYONE:	Come back next year at Obon.

FOLLOW-UP ACTIVITIES

Where in the World Am I? (Geography)

Find Japan on a world map. Locate the major rivers, mountains, and cities and the longitudinal and latitudinal boundaries of Japan.

Make a Flag of Japan (Math, Art)

The Japanese flag is called the **hinomaru** [pronounced hee-no-MAH-roo]. Japan is known as the "Land of the Rising Sun." The red circle on the flag symbolizes the sun. The ratio of the white background width to length is 2:3 (width to length). The red circle in the center has a diameter three-fifths the width of the flag. To make a Japanese flag you will need:

❖ White construction paper, 9 inches by 12 inches

❖ Red construction paper 6 inches square

❖ Compass and pencil

❖ Ruler

❖ Scissors

❖ Glue

Measure, mark, and cut the white paper to a size 8 inches by 12 inches. Using the compass and pencil, draw a 4¾-inch circle on the red paper. Cut the circle out and glue it into the center of the white construction paper. NOTE: Circle diameter will be approximately true to scale.

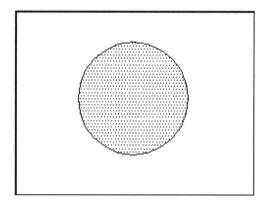

Introduce the equations to calculate diameter, circumference, and area of a circle. Introduce the concept of ratios, and recalculate the flag size both larger and smaller.

The Japanese word for Japan is **Nihon** [pronounced NIH-hon]. It is written with two Chinese characters (called **kanji** by the Japanese). One character, **ni,** means "sun." The second character, **hon,** means "at the base of." Together, Nihon means "at the base of the sun," which can be translated as Land of the Rising Sun.

National Anthem of Japan (Literacy, Music)

The Japanese national anthem is called "Kimigayo" [pronounced kee-mee-GUY-oh]. It is usually sung twice because it is so short. Check the library or look online for a recording. Here are the lyrics:

> May thy peaceful reign last long!
> May it last for thousands of years,
> Until this tiny stone will grow into a massive rock
> And the moss will cover it all deep and thick.

Currency Conversion (Math)

The currency used in Japan is the **yen.** Check an online currency converter or the financial section of a newspaper and compare the value of one Japanese yen to one US dollar. Calculate how much it would cost in yen to buy:

❖ A candy bar (at US $.50)

❖ A pizza (at US $10.00)

❖ A car (at US $15,000.00)

HAVE AN OBON CELEBRATION

Snack on hot green tea, oranges, tangerines, pears, seaweed crackers, and ramen soup. Have students think of someone in their family who has died or bring something to class in remembrance of that person.

Ramen Soup Recipe (Math)

Use packaged dry ramen noodles for a classroom treat. You will need:

- ❖ Ramen noodle soup (allow one package for every 3 or 4 students)
- ❖ Hot water (according to the package)
- ❖ Green onions
- ❖ Soy sauce
- ❖ Measuring spoon
- ❖ Sharp knife
- ❖ Cutting board
- ❖ Crock-pot
- ❖ Ladle
- ❖ Hot-serve paper or Styrofoam cups or bowls
- ❖ Plastic spoons

Wash hands before cooking. Wash green onions and slice them thinly, using the knife and cutting board (this step can be done beforehand, or at home by an adult). Allow approximately 1 tablespoon of green onions and 1 tablespoon soy sauce per package of soup. Following the package directions, place water, noodles, seasoning packet, green onions, and soy sauce into a crock-pot and stir. Soup will be less messy to serve and eat if the dry noodles are crushed slightly before cooking.

Set the crock-pot on its high setting and cook for several hours. (NOTE: If you begin with boiling water, you need to cook only until the ramen noodles are soft.) Ladle into hot-serve paper or Styrofoam cups or bowls.

Create a math activity by recalculating this recipe for the number of packages of ramen noodles made, or do a metric conversion activity. (Refer to the chapter entitled **Measurements and Metric Conversions.**) Make sure the size of the crock-pot will accommodate the number of packages and the water needed.

Paper Fans (Art, Math)

To make paper fans to use in the play and the Obon dance you will need:

- ❖ Plain white 8-½ by 11-inch paper
- ❖ Colored markers or crayons
- ❖ Masking tape

Decorate the paper with a scene from Japan or nature. Then with the paper in front of you, start at one short end and fold the paper, accordion-style. Press hard to crease. Then fold in half, so that it is a double accordion. Wrap the folded end with masking tape to create a handle.

Before you begin to fold, estimate how many folds you will need if each fold is one inch wide. How many if each fold is one-half inch wide? After folding, measure the width of your folds, count the number of folds you made, and check your estimates.

Bon Odori Dance (Physical Education)

Different bon odori dances are performed in different regions of Japan. This one, called the "Coal Miner's Dance," can be danced without music. As students learn the steps, discuss how the movements relate to the work of a coal miner.

1. Form a circle with your left side inside the circle and right side out, holding a paper fan.
2. Step forward on your right foot. At the same time, make a downward shoveling motion to the right with your hands.
3. Step forward on your left foot and make a shoveling motion with your hands to the left.
4. Step forward on your right foot and pretend to throw a shovel load over your right shoulder.
5. Repeat with your left foot and throw a shovel load over your left shoulder.
6. Step back on your left foot. Raise your right hand in front of your face and lower your left hand down beside your left leg. Then step back on your right foot, raising your left hand in front of your face and lowering your right hand down beside your right leg.
7. Step forward on your right foot while pushing your hands forward, as if pushing a coal cart. Repeat, as you step forward on your left foot.
8. Step forward on your right foot and cross your arms over each other in front of your body in a scissors motion.
9. Clap three times (fast-fast, slow).
10. Repeat entire sequence.

While dancers perform the bon odori, a drummer in the center of the dance circle plays a large, double-sided drum. The drum is beaten with two wooden sticks. Students can use a plastic bucket and sturdy rulers or sticks to simulate a taiko.

Paper Lanterns (Art)

To make paper lanterns as props for the play, you will need:

- ❖ 1 sheet of 9-inch by 12-inch construction paper (any color)
- ❖ Ruler
- ❖ Scissors
- ❖ Tape
- ❖ Hole punch
- ❖ 12 inches of string

Fold the paper lengthwise and then in half from bottom to top. Then fold the paper again lengthwise and again in half from bottom to top. Cut small snips from the four edges of the paper. When you open the paper, you will have a cut-out pattern, similar to making paper snowflakes. Roll the paper lengthwise into a cylinder and tape the ends to form your lantern. Using a hole punch, make a hole at the top edge of each side of your lantern. Thread the string through the holes and tie the ends of the string together for a handle.

Toro Nagashi Boats (Science, Art)

Toro Nagashi is the lantern floating ceremony at the end of Obon. At that time, small boats made from straw or wood are floated on a lake, river, or ocean. Small lanterns are placed on the boats. The ceremony guides the ancestors' spirits back from this world to theirs. To make a boat you will need:

- ❖ 1 empty and clean half-gallon milk carton
- ❖ 1 empty and clean half-pint milk carton
- ❖ Scissors
- ❖ Tea light (candle)
- ❖ Ruler
- ❖ Pen
- ❖ Strapping tape
- ❖ Stickers or waterproof, sticky-backed decorative plastic (optional)

With scissors, cut off and discard the tops of the milk cartons. Set the small carton to one side. Cut off and discard the bottom of the large carton. Cut down one edge of the carton and open it flat. Cut as shown and refold the carton so that you end up with a U-shaped piece with short, 1-inch sides.

At this point, you may decorate the boat bottom and the small milk carton, if desired, with stickers or waterproof, sticky-backed decorative plastic.

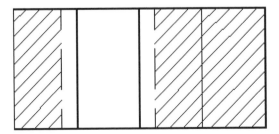
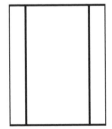

Lap a strip of strapping tape approximately 3 inches long over itself to create a loop of tape with the sticky side out. Place it on the bottom of the small milk carton. Place the small milk carton in the approximate center of the boat base and press to attach the small milk carton to the boat bottom.

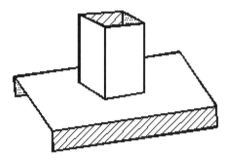

Make a smaller loop of tape with a 2-inch strip of strapping tape and attach the tea light to the inside center of the small milk carton. NOTE: The tea light can be eliminated if the lanterns will not be lit and floated as a classroom activity.

Float the boats in a sink or large tub of water. Discuss some or all of the following:

❖ The need for stabilization in wind or moving water—by using a rudder or by the design of this boat.

❖ Introduce the concept of **displacement.** Discuss how large ocean liners are made of extremely heavy metal. Explain how a chunk of metal placed in water would sink to the bottom, but that dense substances can be reshaped to increase the amount of water they displace.

Haiku (Literacy, Language Arts)

The Japanese poetic form called **haiku** [pronounced HIGH-koo] was developed in the sixteenth century. Basho Matsuo was one of the first great Japanese haiku poets. Locate and read some of Basho's haiku poetry and have students write their own.

Haiku does not need to rhyme, but it has a specific structure. Haiku consists of 3 lines in which the number of syllables is important. The typical syllable pattern is 5-7-5, meaning that the first line contains 5 syllables, the second line contains 7 syllables, and the third line contains 5 syllables.

The subjects of haiku are generally images from nature and everyday life. Haiku is usually told in the present tense, and each line should stand alone—not running over into the next line, as in other forms of poetry. Try to include senses (sight, sound, smell, taste, touch, movement). Examples of subjects for a haiku might include the way a cloud moves, the sound of leaves in a tree, raindrops falling into a puddle, or the movement of a butterfly.

Japanese Phrases (Literacy, Language Arts)

The Japanese "r" sound is very soft—almost a cross between an "r" and an "l." Learn a few Japanese phrases. This is how they might look in English, how they are pronounced, and what they mean:

English Writing	Pronunciation	Meaning
Konnichiwa	kon-nee-chee-WAH	Hello
O-genki desu ka?	oh-GEN-kee dess-KAH?	How are you?
Onegai shimasu	oh-neh-guy shee-mah-sh	Please
Domo arigato	doh-moh ah-ree-GAH-toh	Thank you
Do itashi mashite	doh EE-tah-shee mah-sh-teh	You're welcome
Sayonara	sa-YOH-nah-rah	Goodbye

SUGGESTIONS FOR FURTHER ACTIVITIES

History/Political Science: Research Japan's form of government as a constitutional monarchy with a parliamentary government. Compare this form of government with ours. What other countries in the world have a form of government similar to Japan's?

Science: Discuss a lunar month and how it relates to a month of our calendar. (See the chapter entitled **Calendars.**)

Science: Discuss why fish, seafood, and other items from the sea are such an important part of the Japanese diet. Relate diet to the natural resources and geography of Japan. Research the type of fishing and ocean harvesting used in Japan.

Science: Japan has about 1500 seismic occurrences every year. Discuss plate tectonics and earthquake fault lines. Discuss why we might use a Japanese word—**tsunami**—to describe catastrophic waves and why the Japanese would have a special word for this kind of wave. What is the relationship between earthquakes and tsunamis?

Math: Origami—Japanese paper folding—originally came from China. Learn to make some simple origami objects. (See the **April** chapter for instructions for making an origami frog.) Discuss the geometry of making a square from a rectangle and a triangle from a square.

September—Homowo

(Ghana)

BACKGROUND

The Ga people migrated to the west coast of Africa, near the country now called Ghana. Along the way, they ran out of food. But because they helped each other, they survived. After they settled in their new home, they held a feast at harvest time to remember their difficult migration and to laugh at hunger. The festival known as Homowo—"hunger hooting"—reenacts the migration and first harvest. It is sometimes called the Yam Festival, because yams are one of the main foods of the people of Ghana. Homowo is celebrated at harvest time, in August or September.

READERS THEATRE SCRIPT—HOOTING AT HUNGER!

Suggested Costumes and Props

❖ Lengths of fabric draped under the right arm and tied at the left shoulder (Scenes 1, 2, 3, 4, and 5)

❖ Poles for walking sticks (Scenes 1, 2, and 3)

❖ Bundles and baskets (Scenes 1, 2, and 3)

❖ Baskets of plastic fruit and vegetables (Scenes 4 and 5)

Characters

The following is a list of characters. Consider having different Narrators for ancient Ghana, modern Ghana, and Scene 5.

- NARRATOR 1
- NARRATOR 2
- KING
- QUEEN
- TRAVELER
- VILLAGER 1
- VILLAGER 2
- VILLAGER 3
- VILLAGER 4
- ADDO

- KAYA
- MODERN VILLAGER 1
- MODERN VILLAGER 2
- MODERN VILLAGER 3
- MODERN VILLAGER 4
- TEACHER
- STUDENT 1
- STUDENT 2
- STUDENT 3
- STUDENT 4

Presentation Suggestions

This play includes 5 scenes. Narrator 1 and Narrator 2 will be onstage at all times. Decorate the back of the stage with a backdrop, made from butcher paper, that depicts a landscape, or with individual flags of Ghana made by students. The **SETTING** at the beginning of each scene is to assist the characters and is not intended to be read. Performance suggestions (gestures, movements, facial expressions) and pronunciation helps are included in brackets.

Hooting at Hunger!

Scene 1—The Journey Begins

SETTING: The time before the Ga migration, in a Ga village. Onstage are Narrator 1, Narrator 2, the Ga King, the Ga Queen, Traveler, Villager 1, Villager 2, Villager 3, and Villager 4.

NARRATOR 1:	The Ga people live in western Africa, in the country known as Ghana.
NARRATOR 2:	But the ancient Ga lived near the land we now call Nigeria.
NARRATOR 1:	The holiday called Homowo relives their journey to their new country.
NARRATOR 2:	Let's go back in time to the migration.
VILLAGER 1:	Look—the traveler from our village has returned!
TRAVELER:	It is good to be home.
KING:	What did you see on your travels?
TRAVELER:	To the west there is a great land!
KING:	What is it like?
TRAVELER:	There is good soil.
VILLAGER 2:	We could plant our crops there.
TRAVELER:	There are few people there.
VILLAGER 3:	We wouldn't have to share our land.
TRAVELER:	There is also an ocean filled with fish.
VILLAGER 4:	Fish to eat!
QUEEN:	Is the land better than here?
TRAVELER:	We could have a good life there.
KING:	Everyone pack up and let's head out.
VILLAGER 1:	Where are we going?
KING:	West—toward the ocean.
QUEEN:	West—toward the setting sun.

KING: West—to our new home.

NARRATOR 1:   The Ga people packed up their belongings.

NARRATOR 2:   They packed food for the long journey.

NARRATOR 1:   And they headed west.

Scene 2—Along the Way

SETTING: On the journey. Onstage are Narrator 1, Narrator 2, the King, the Queen, Traveler, and Villagers 1, 2, 3, and 4.

NARRATOR 1:   The Ga people traveled west.

NARRATOR 2:   It was hard to travel with so many people.

NARRATOR 1:   They had to stay together.

NARRATOR 2:   And they had to carry everything they owned.

[Except for Narrator 1 and Narrator 2, characters walk back and forth across the stage a few times and then stop]

KING: Let's stop here.

VILLAGER 1:   We can rest.

VILLAGER 2:   And gather food.

VILLAGER 2:   And more water.

VILLAGER 4:   We'll need it to finish our journey.

NARRATOR 1:   The Ga people rested and found more food and water.

NARRATOR 2:   Then they continued west once more.

KING: Let's go.

[The characters walk back and forth across the stage a few times and then stop]

NARRATOR 1:   It was a long journey.

NARRATOR 2:   Finally the Ga people ran out of food.

NARRATOR 1:   They couldn't find any more food along the way.

NARRATOR 2:   They began to starve.

VILLAGER 1:   We are tired.

VILLAGER 2:   We have no food.

KING: Do you want to just sit here and die?

VILLAGER 3:	No!
VILLAGER 3:	But we need food!
KING:	I smell something.
QUEEN:	What do you smell?
KING:	The air—it smells different.
QUEEN:	Yes, it smells clean and salty.
TRAVELER:	That's fresh air from the ocean you smell!
KING:	We're close to the ocean?
TRAVELER:	Yes! It's just a little further.
KING:	Let's go. We can make it.
VILLAGER 1:	Why should we?
VILLAGER 2:	I'm tired.
VILLAGER 3:	I'm hungry.
VILLAGER 4:	We might as well just die here.
VILLAGER 1:	That would save us the walking.
TRAVELER:	But the ocean is filled with fish!
VILLAGER 2:	Fish?
VILLAGER 3:	To eat?
KING:	Let's go everyone.
QUEEN:	Did you hear people? There's fish to eat.
VILLAGER 4:	Okay. Let's go.
NARRATOR 1:	The Ga people finally made it to their new home.
NARRATOR 2:	They found food to eat, and they lived.

Scene 3—The First Homowo Festival

SETTING: Ghana. Onstage are Narrator 1, Narrator 2, King, Queen, Explorer, Villager 1, Villager 2, Villager 3, and Villager 4.

NARRATOR 1:	The journey had taught the Ga people a lesson.
NARRATOR 2:	They knew what it was like to be hungry.
NARRATOR 1:	They also knew something else.

NARRATOR 2:	They knew they never wanted to be hungry again.
KING:	This is a great place.
QUEEN:	Yes! I like it much better here than our old homeland.
VILLAGER 1:	But I never want to be hungry again.
KING:	No, that was bad!
VILLAGER 2:	What can we do?
VILLAGER 3:	Even living here, we might still go hungry one day.
QUEEN:	There must be something we can do.
KING:	Let's plant crops.
VILLAGER 4:	Let's plant lots of crops.
VILLAGER 1:	Lots and lots of crops!
VILLAGER 2:	And let's work together.
VILLAGER 3:	And let's have a plan for our crops.
VILLAGER 4:	Then we'll never go hungry again.
NARRATOR 1:	So the Ga people started a big agricultural program.
NARRATOR 2:	They worked hard and planted many crops.
NARRATOR 1:	Their first harvest was huge.
NARRATOR 2:	They had plenty of food.
NARRATOR 1:	Because they worked together.

Scene 4—Modern Day Homowo Festival

SETTING: A village in modern Ghana. Onstage are Narrator 1, Narrator 2, Addo, Kaya, and Villagers 1, 2, 3, and 4.

NARRATOR 1:	Today the people in Ghana reenact the migration of the Ga people.
NARRATOR 2:	They celebrate the first harvest in their new homeland.
NARRATOR 1:	Children often play the parts of the Ga people.
NARRATOR 2:	Let's see what a celebration might look like.
VILLAGER 1:	It's time for the procession.
VILLAGER 2:	Yes! Let's reenact the time our people came to Ghana.
VILLAGER 3:	Who is our Ga King?

ADDO: I get to be the Ga King this year.

VILLAGER 4: Good for you, Addo.

VILLAGER 1: Who will play the part of our Ga Queen?

KAYA: I'm the Ga Queen!

VILLAGER 2: You'll be a good Ga Queen, Kaya.

KAYA: Thank you, but why do you say that?

VILLAGER 3: Because your name means, "stay and don't go back."

KAYA: Oh, that's right! I AM the perfect Ga Queen.

VILLAGER 4: Yes, because the Ga Queen moved to her new home and didn't go back.

ADDO: That's what all the other Ga people did, too.

VILLAGER 1: Right! They all moved and didn't go back.

VILLAGER 2: Let's start our procession then.

VILLAGER 3: King Addo—get us started.

ADDO (KING): Let's go, people—west, toward the setting sun.

[Except for Narrator 1 and Narrator 2, all the characters walk back and forth across the stage and then stop]

VILLAGER 1: I'm hungry.

VILLAGER 2: Are we there yet?

VILLAGER 3: I'm really hungry.

VILLAGER 4: We're all hungry!

KAYA (QUEEN): We'll make it—just a little farther.

VILLAGER 1: We made it.

VILLAGER 2: Our new home.

VILLAGER 3: There's plenty of food here.

VILLAGER 4: But I never want to be hungry again.

ADDO (KING): Let's plant crops.

VILLAGER 1: Let's plant lots of crops.

VILLAGER 2: Enough so we'll never go hungry.

KAYA (QUEEN): Then we can hoot at hunger!

NARRATOR 1: And that's what the people of Ga did after their first harvest.

NARRATOR 2: They hooted at hunger!

NARRATOR 1: Today, they celebrate that time with the Homowo Festival.

NARRATOR 2: Homowo means "hunger-hooting" festival.

[Everyone onstage]: Hoot! Hoot! Hoot! Hoot!

Scene 5—Modern American Classroom

SETTING: American class discussing the yam festival. Onstage are Narrator 1, Narrator 2, Teacher, and Students 1, 2, 3, and 4.

NARRATOR 1: Yams are one of the most important foods in Ghana.

NARRATOR 2: The people of Ghana eat them almost every day.

NARRATOR 1: Because yams are such an important food…

NARRATOR 2: …the Homowo festival is sometimes called the "yam festival."

NARRATOR 1: Now let's listen in on a classroom in America talking about Homowo.

TEACHER: What did you learn about Homowo?

STUDENT 1: I learned that the festival includes a feast.

STUDENT 2: Just like our Thanksgiving.

STUDENT 3: I learned that people who have moved away often return home for the festival.

STUDENT 2: Just like our Thanksgiving.

STUDENT 4: I learned that yams are an important part of this holiday feast.

STUDENT 2: Just like our Thanksgiving.

STUDENT 1: I learned that the Ga people left their homeland to make a better life for themselves in a new land.

STUDENT 2: Just like the settlers did before our first Thanksgiving.

STUDENT 3: I learned that the Ga people almost died from hunger when they moved to their new land.

STUDENT 2: Just like the first settlers did when they moved to America.

STUDENT 4: I learned that the Ga people celebrated having lots of food after the first harvest in their new home.

STUDENT 2: Just like the early settlers did in America.

STUDENT 1: I learned that Homowo celebrates abundance.

STUDENT 3: So twins are honored by being smeared with white paint and dressed in white clothes.

STUDENT 2: Just like—hey, THAT's different!

STUDENT 4: And the Ga people celebrate by hooting at hunger!

STUDENT 2: That's REALLY different! But it's a great idea!

[Everyone onstage]: Hoot! Hoot! Hoot! Hoot!

FOLLOW-UP ACTIVITIES

Where in the World Am I? (Geography)

Find Ghana on a world map. Locate the major rivers, lakes, mountains, and Accra—the capital of Ghana. Find the longitudinal and latitudinal boundaries of Ghana.

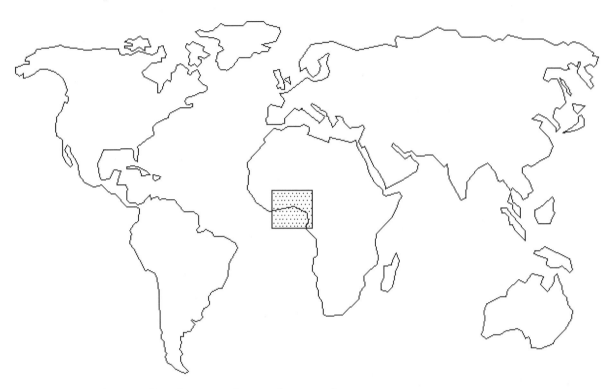

Make a Flag of Ghana (Math, Art)

The red, black, and green of the Ghana flag are called "Pan-African colors." These colors are found on the flags of many African nations to show their unity. The black star in the center of the Ghana flag represents the fact that Ghana was the first independent African nation of the twentieth century. The red represents the blood of those who died for the country. Gold represents the mineral gold, which is a source of wealth for Ghana. Green represents the country's forests. To make a flag of Ghana you will need:

❖ One sheet of 9-inch by 12-inch red construction paper

❖ One sheet of 9-inch by 12-inch green construction paper

❖ One sheet of 9-inch by 12-inch yellow construction paper

❖ Black construction paper

❖ Star template, photocopied

❖ Pencil

❖ Scissors

❖ Glue

❖ Paper cutter, or ruler and scissors

The ratio of the flag of Ghana is 2:3 (width to length). Using a ruler, pencil, and scissors, measure, mark, and cut the yellow paper to a size 8 inches by 12 inches. Then measure, mark, and cut strips of the red and green construction paper 2½ inches by 12 inches. Measure, mark, and cut a piece of black paper to a size 4 inches square. NOTE: A paper cutter can be used ahead of time. However, consider having students work in groups to measure, cut, and share paper for the additional mathematics tie-in.

Lay the yellow sheet of paper horizontally in front of you. Glue one red piece of paper horizontally to the top of the yellow paper, matching the edges. Glue one green piece of paper horizontally to the bottom of the yellow paper, matching the edges. the capital of Ghana. Find the longitudinal and latitudinal boundaries of Ghana.

Trace the star template onto black construction paper. Cut out and glue the star in the center of the yellow section of the flag, with one tip of the star pointing to the top of the flag.

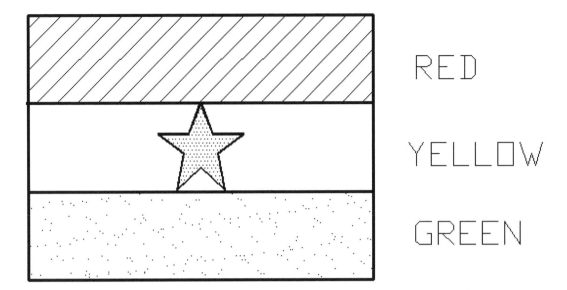

RED

YELLOW

GREEN

NOTE: The stripes and star size will be approximate in relation to the official ratio. For an additional math activity, recalculate the size of the star and measurements for the stripes based on the true ratio for a larger size and a smaller size flag.

National Anthem of Ghana (Literacy, Music)

The national anthem of Ghana is called "Hail the Name of Ghana." Check the library or look online for a recording. Read and discuss the Ghana National Anthem. The following is a portion of it:

God bless our homeland Ghana
And make our nation great and strong,
Bold to defend forever
The cause of Freedom and of Right;
Fill our hearts with true humility,
Make us cherish fearless honesty,
And help us to resist oppressors' rule
With all our will and might evermore.

Currency Conversion (Math)

The currency of Ghana is called the cedi [pronounced SAY-dee] (sometimes listed as GHC). Locate an online currency converter or the financial section of the newspaper and calculate how much it would cost in each country's currency to buy:

❖ A candy bar (at US $.50)

❖ A pizza (at US $10.00)

❖ A car (at US $15,000.00)

HAVE A HOMOWO CELEBRATION

Yam Foofoo Recipe (Math)

Here is a recipe for foofoo, a popular dish in Ghana made from yams. To make enough foofoo to serve approximately 10, you will need:

- ❖ 1 pounds yams
- ❖ ¼ teaspoon black pepper
- ❖ ¼ teaspoon salt
- ❖ 1 teaspoon butter
- ❖ Large pot with cover and heating source, or electric crock-pot
- ❖ Measuring spoons
- ❖ Potato masher, wooden spoon, or electric mixer
- ❖ Serving platter

Wash hands before cooking. Place yams in cold water. Bring to boil and cook for 25 minutes, until soft. Let yams cool slightly, then peel. Mash with the remaining ingredients—using a potato masher, wooden spoon, or electric mixer—until completely smooth. Foofoo will be slightly sticky. Roll into balls about 1 inch in diameter and place on serving plate. Serve warm.

Calculate how many servings are needed for the class and use this recipe as a math activity to double or triple the recipe. Refer to the chapter entitled **Measurements and Metric Conversions.**

Hot Plantain Crisp Recipe (Math)

Have you ever seen hard, greenish-yellow bananas, called **plantains** [pronounced plan-TANES], at the grocery store? They are a type of cooking banana grown in many tropical parts of the world. To make 16 to 20 appetizers, you will need:

- ❖ 2 firm plantains
- ❖ 2 teaspoons lemon juice
- ❖ 2 teaspoons ground ginger
- ❖ 2 teaspoons cayenne pepper
- ❖ Oil for frying
- ❖ Sharp knife
- ❖ Cutting board
- ❖ Mixing bowl
- ❖ Measuring spoons
- ❖ Mixing spoon
- ❖ Small bowl

❖ Electric skillet

❖ Spatula for turning

❖ Serving plate

❖ Paper towels

Wash hands before cooking. Peel plantains and slice into ½-inch-thick rounds. Place in mixing bowl, sprinkle with lemon juice, and toss. Combine ginger and pepper in small bowl.

Pour enough oil in skillet to cover bottom of pan ¼-inch deep. Heat until a drop of water in the oil sizzles. Roll plantain slices in spices and fry until the outsides are crisp and golden. Dry on paper towel and serve hot.

Hydroelectric Power (Geography, Science)

Ghana is located a few degrees north of the Equator. (See the chapter entitled **Latitude and Longitude.**) The climate is tropical. Ghana's tropical rainforest is broken by heavily forested hills, streams, rivers, grassy plains, and low bush. Lake Volta, located in Ghana, is the largest man-made lake in the world. It generates electricity and is a source of water for irrigation and fish farming.

To understand how water can be a source of energy, try this simple experiment. You will need a plastic pinwheel and a hose or water faucet. Hold the pinwheel under a stream of water. As the water hits the pinwheel, the force of the water causes the pinwheel to turn. What is happening? Moving water has *inertia*, which means it tends to keep moving and applies force against anything that is in its way.

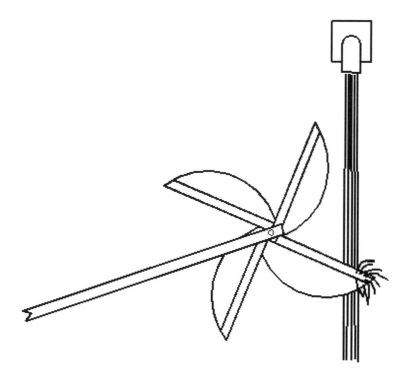

The faster the water moves, the more force it has. Large bodies of water, such as Lake Volta, can use this principle of science in a way that is similar to the pinwheel spinning under a stream of water. To create hydroelectricity, a dam at one end of the lake blocks the flow of the water. The water at the surface pushes down on the water at the bottom, which builds up even more pressure as water keeps coming toward the dam without being able to flow out. At the very bottom of the dam, pipes permit the built-up water to rush through and turn giant wheels called *turbines*. These turbines then operate generators, which create electrical current.

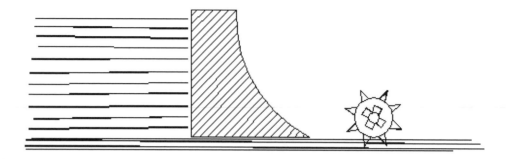

Adinkra Cloth (Math, Science, Art)

Adinkra [pronounced ah-DEEN-krah] cloth is hand-printed by the Ashanti tribe in Ghana, and it is traditionally made for Ashanti royalty to wear during religious ceremonies. The Ashanti people create a dye from bark, which they use to stamp designs carved from gourds onto fabric. They first draw lines onto the cloth with the dye to divide the cloth into squares. The gourds are then carved with designs, dipped into the dye, and stamped onto the fabric. To print adinkra cloth designs on paper you will need:

❖ Paper grocery bag (cut open, and with the bottom removed) or construction paper

❖ Paint

❖ Pencil or marker

❖ Small tray for paint

❖ Potato

❖ Sharp knife (for adult)

❖ Plastic knife (for student)

Ahead of time, cut the potatoes so each student has half a potato to use as a stamp. Students create a design with paper and pencil. Then, using a plastic knife, they carve that design into the cut end of the potato. Carve AWAY portions of the potato so that a 3-dimensional design remains. Dip the design end into paint and press it onto the paper. Students may wish to share their potato stamps for variety.

Students may use the following figures for inspiration or create some of their own. These symbols have certain meanings to the people of Ghana. From left to right they are: a heart that reminds us to learn from our past; a symbol to remind us about friendship and sharing; the moon and star to symbolize faithfulness; and the ram's head to symbolize strength, wisdom, and learning.

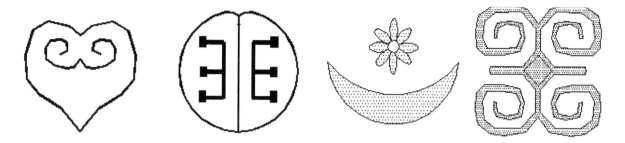

Compare the style of these symbols with those of other cultures—such as the ancient Mayans, Egyptians, and early Native American Indians—who also used pictures to tell stories. As students are working, introduce and discuss the concept of symmetry in these designs.

Play a Folk Game from Ghana (Physical Education)

Children in Ghana sometimes play a game similar to our game of "Button, button, who's got the button." The name of this folk game means, "It was not put behind you."

To play, all students except one (Student A, who is "it") sit in a circle. Student A runs around the outside of the circle, carrying a small cloth. The students in the circle are not allowed to look behind them. Student A silently drops the cloth behind one of the seated students (Student B) but continues to run around the circle as if he hadn't dropped it.

The object is for Student B to recognize that the cloth is there, pick it up, and chase after Student A, tagging Student A before Student A has a chance to sit down in Student B's place. If Student A successfully sits down before being tagged, Student B is the new "it." If Student B tags Student A before Student A can sit, then Student A remains "it." The game continues until the players decide to stop.

SUGGESTIONS FOR FURTHER ACTIVITIES

History: Ghana became a self-governing country in 1957, when it gained independence from Great Britain. Research how Ghana went from a British colony to an independent nation. Compare and contrast the process with that of the United States, also a former British colony.

Social Studies: The government of Ghana is a constitutional democracy. Research this type of government. What other countries have a similar form of government?

Literacy: Anansi the Spider is a character found in many Ashanti stories. Find and read a retelling of an Anansi story.

Language Arts: Have students write a poem or story about working together, or relate a time when they did or did not work together well with others.

Science: Research yams—what the plant looks like and what type of climate it needs. Discuss yams as an important food in Ghana. Compare yams to potatoes in the Irish diet and rice in many Asian diets.

Science: One of Ghana's natural resources is industrial diamonds. Research how diamonds are created, what industrial diamonds are used for, and how they are similar to—and different from—precious diamonds.

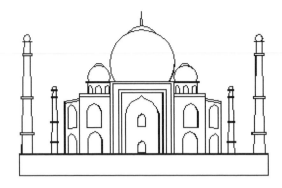

October—Divali

(India)

BACKGROUND

Divali [pronounced dih-VAH-lee], a Hindu religious holiday known as the Festival of Lights, begins the East Indian New Year. Hindus believe that Lakshmi, the goddess of prosperity, visits homes lit by lamps. The word *Divali* comes from the word *deepavali*, which means "row of lamps." The festival represents the triumph of light over darkness and good over evil. The holiday is celebrated in October or November, depending on the lunar calendar.

READERS THEATRE SCRIPT—FESTIVAL OF LIGHTS

Suggested Costumes and Props

- ❖ Book for business accounts
- ❖ 2 flowers — one for each of Lakshmi's 2 top hands

Characters

The following is a list of characters.

- NARRATOR 1
- NARRATOR 2
- KING DASARTHA
- LORD RAMA
- QUEEN KAIKAYEE
- LAKSHMAN
- SITA
- DEMON KING RAVANA

- PEOPLE OF THE KINGDOM OF AYODHYA
- GODDESS LAKSHMI
- PEOPLE TALKING TO GODDESS
- AJAY
- SHANTI
- MODERN MOTHER
- MODERN FATHER

Presentation Suggestions

This play includes 6 scenes. Narrator 1 and Narrator 2 will be onstage at all times. Decorate the stage with a butcher paper backdrop depicting a landscape, or with individual flags of India made by students. The **SETTING** at the beginning of each scene is to assist the characters and is not intended to be read. Performance suggestions (gestures, movements, facial expressions) and pronunciation helps are included in brackets.

Festival of Lights

Scene 1—King Dasartha

SETTING: Ancient India, in the palace of King Dasartha. Onstage are Narrator 1, Narrator 2, King Dasartha, his son Rama, and Rama's stepmother, Queen Kaikayee.

NARRATOR 1:	Divali is a holiday celebrated in India.
NARRATOR 2:	It is called a Festival of Lights.
NARRATOR 1:	There are many legends about how Divali began.
NARRATOR 2:	Here is one of them.
NARRATOR 1:	Long ago in northern India, there was a king.
NARRATOR 2:	His name was King Dasartha.
	[pronounced DUSH-rath]
NARRATOR 1:	The king had many sons and many wives.
NARRATOR 2:	One of his sons was named Rama.
	[pronounced RAH-mah or RAHM]
NARRATOR 1:	One of his wives was named Queen Kaikayee.
	[pronounced KEH-ka-hee]
NARRATOR 2:	Queen Kaikayee was Rama's stepmother.
KING:	Rama, my son. You are wise and kind.
RAMA:	Thank you, Father. I hope I will be a wise and kind king one day.
QUEEN KAIKAYEE:	What makes you think you'll be king, Rama?
RAMA:	Why wouldn't I be king, Stepmother?
QUEEN:	You're not the only prince. My son is a prince, too.
NARRATOR 1:	Every mother wants the best for her children.
NARRATOR 2:	The queen wanted her son to be king.
NARRATOR 1:	Too bad for Rama.
NARRATOR 2:	The queen's selfishness turned the king away from Rama.

From *Around the World Through Holidays: Cross Curricular Readers Theatre* written and illustrated by Carol Peterson. Westport, CT: Teacher Ideas Press/Libraries Unlimited. Copyright © 2006.

KING:	Rama, for peace in my household, you must leave.
RAMA:	But I was to succeed you as king and rule the kingdom.
KING:	I'm sorry, son.
RAMA:	As you wish, Father. I shall take my wife, Sita, and my brother, Lakshman, with me.
	[pronounced SEE-tah; and LOOKSH-mun]
KING:	Good luck to you all.
NARRATOR 1:	And so, Rama and his wife and brother left the palace.
NARRATOR 2:	They went into the countryside of India.

Scene 2—Exile

SETTING: Ancient Indian countryside. Onstage are Narrator 1, Narrator 2, Rama, Sita, Lakshman. At the end of the scene, the evil King Ravana is onstage.

NARRATOR 1:	Rama left his father's kingdom.
NARRATOR 2:	His younger brother, Lakshman, went with him.
NARRATOR 1:	So did Rama's wife, Sita.
NARRATOR 2:	Sita was beautiful.
NARRATOR 1:	No she wasn't.
NARRATOR 2:	Sita *wasn't* beautiful?
NARRATOR 1:	No. She was *very* beautiful.
NARRATOR 2:	Okay. So Rama, Lakshman, and the *very beautiful* Sita roamed the countryside.
	[Rama, Lakshman, and Sita walk across the stage]
NARRATOR 1:	One day, King Ravana saw Sita.
	[pronounced RAH-vun]
	[King Ravana enters from stage left or stage right]
NARRATOR 2:	King Ravana was a demon with 10 heads.
NARRATOR 1:	A demon?
NARRATOR 2:	Yes! An evil demon!
RAVANA:	Oh, that woman is beautiful! I want her for my wife.
NARRATOR 1:	But Rama and Lakshman were always with Sita.

NARRATOR 2:	Until one day when Rama and Lakshman left her alone.
	[Rama and Lakshman exit stage left or stage right]
RAVANA:	Now's my chance to grab Sita. I'll wear a disguise.
NARRATOR 1:	Ravana disguised himself as a beggar.
RAVANA:	Please help me.
NARRATOR 2:	Sita was not only beautiful—she was kind, too.
SITA:	[approaching Ravana] What do you need?
NARRATOR 2:	When Sita came close to Ravana, he captured her.
	[Ravana grasps Sita by the arm]
SITA:	Help! Save me!
NARRATOR 1:	But Rama and Lakshman were gone.
NARRATOR 1:	Ravana took Sita to his kingdom of Lanka.
	[pronounced LAHN-kah]

Scene 3—The Battle for Sita

SETTING: The ancient Indian countryside. Onstage are Narrator 1, Narrator 2, Rama, Lakshman, Sita, and King Ravana. Sita and King Ravana are off to one side.

NARRATOR 1:	When Rama and Lakshman returned, Sita was gone.
NARRATOR 2:	They knew she had been taken by the demon king.
NARRATOR 1:	Rama and Lakshman searched for Sita.
	[Rama and Lakshman walk across the stage]
NARRATOR 2:	They finally came to King Ravana's kingdom.
RAMA:	Sita! There you are!
LAKSHMAN:	Are you all right?
SITA:	Help me! Evil King Ravana has captured me.
RAMA:	We'll save you.
NARRATOR 1:	Rama and Lakshman fought the evil 10-headed demon king for 10 days.
	[Rama, Lakshman, and Ravana fight]
NARRATOR 2:	Finally Rama and Lakshman killed the demon king.
	[Ravana falls to the ground]

NARRATOR 1:	And rescued Sita.
SITA:	You saved me!
LAKSHMAN:	Let's go home. We've been gone 14 years.
RAMA:	You're right—we defeated the demon king. We deserve to go home.

[Rama, Sita, and Lakshman walk across the stage]

NARRATOR 2:	So Rama, Sita, and Lakshman set off to return to their kingdom.

Scene 4—The Return of Rama

SETTING: The kingdom of King Dasartha. Onstage are Narrator 1, Narrator 2, and Villagers 1, 2, 3, and 4. Later Rama, Sita, and Lakshman enter from stage left or stage right.

NARRATOR 1:	The people in King Dasartha's kingdom heard that Rama was returning.
NARRATOR 1:	They were happy.
VILLAGER 1:	Good news! Remember Rama?
VILLAGER 2:	Yes. Rama was a wise and kind prince.
VILLAGER 1:	He's coming home.
VILLAGER 3:	Are Sita and Lakshman coming home, too?
VILLAGER 1:	Yes. Rama killed the evil King Ravana!
VILLAGER 4:	That's great news!
VILLAGER 1:	But look. It's getting dark.
VILLAGER 2:	How will Lord Rama find his way home in the dark?
VILLAGER 3:	Let's light lamps for him.
VILLAGER 4:	Let's light every lamp we have.
VILLAGER 1:	Then he can see his way home.

[Rama, Sita, and Lakshman enter from stage left or stage right. Villagers cheer]

VILLAGER 2:	Welcome home, Lord Rama.
VILLAGER 3:	We heard you killed the evil King Ravana.
VILLAGER 4:	Tell us about it.

NARRATOR 1: Rama told the people all about his victory over evil.

NARRATOR 2: The people wanted to celebrate.

VILLAGER 1: Let's light lamps every year at this time to remember Lord Rama's victory over evil.

VILLAGER 2: Let's remember that truth and goodness are like light.

VILLAGER 3: And evil is like darkness.

VILLAGER 4: The lights will remind us that goodness defeats the darkness of evil.

NARRATOR 1: Rama rid the world of the evil demon.

NARRATOR 2: Then he ruled the kingdom with wisdom and kindness.

NARRATOR 1: Because of Rama, the people of India began to celebrate each year.

NARRATOR 2: They called the celebration Divali.

NARRATOR 2: Divali is a festival of light.

NARRATOR 1: Divali comes from the word *deepavali*.

NARRATOR 2: Deepavali means "row of lamps".

NARRATOR 1: Divali occurs during the lunar New Year for Indians.

NARRATOR 2: It celebrates new beginnings.

Scene 5—The Goddess Lakshmi

SETTING: Ancient Indian village. On stage are Narrator 1, Narrator 2, the goddess Lakshmi (2 students—one nonspeaking), and Villagers 1, 2, 3, and 4.

NARRATOR 1: People in India who are of the Hindu religion believe in many gods and goddesses.

NARRATOR 2: One of their goddesses is Lakshmi.

[pronounced LOOKSH-mee]

NARRATOR 1: They believe Lakshmi was born at the same time of the year that Divali is celebrated.

NARRATOR 2: So she is often worshipped during Divali.

[Have 2 students portray Lakshmi—one standing in front of the other to portray the goddess as having four arms]

NARRATOR 1: Let's meet Lakshmi.

VILLAGER 1:	Hello, goddess Lakshmi.
VILLAGER 2:	Where did you come from?
LAKSHMI:	I was born in the ocean on a lotus flower.
VILLAGER 1:	What are you holding?
LAKSHMI:	I carry lotus flowers in two of my hands.
VILLAGER 2:	Why?
LAKSHMI:	The lotus flower represents a sinless mind.
VILLAGER 3:	But your other two hands are empty.
LAKSHMI:	That is to remind you that you come into the world with nothing and you leave with nothing.
VILLAGER 4:	What about when we are alive?
LAKSHMI:	By giving to others who need it, your wealth will increase.
VILLAGER 1:	So you are the goddess of fortune.
LAKSHMI:	I am also the goddess of peace, health, friends, family, long life, and knowledge.
VILLAGER 2:	Knowledge?
LAKSHMI:	Knowledge is the ultimate wealth.
VILLAGER 3:	Why?
LAKSHMI:	Because it cannot be stolen from you. Knowledge is also the ultimate strength.
VILLAGER 4:	Why?
LAKSHMI:	Because a smart person can often defeat physical force.
VILLAGER 1:	You are wise, Lakshmi.
VILLAGER 2:	And beautiful.
VILLAGER 3:	And kind.
VILLAGER 4:	And good.

Scene 6—A Modern Divali

SETTING: A home in modern-day India. Onstage are Narrator 1, Narrator 2, Ajay, his sister Shanti, their father, and their mother. [names are pronounced AY-jay; SHAWN-tee]

NARRATOR 1:	Let's see how a family might celebrate Divali today.
AJAY:	It's almost time for Divali.

MOTHER:	Let's decorate our statue of the goddess Lakshmi.
SHANTI:	I've picked some flowers to decorate her statue.
AJAY:	I've bought some candy and fruit to place in front her statue.
SHANTI:	Father, how will you honor Lakshmi?
FATHER:	I will balance the account books for my business.
AJAY:	How will that honor Lakshmi?
FATHER:	It will make sure our business is in order for the New Year.
MOTHER:	We'll ask Lakshmi to bring us good fortune.
SHANTI:	Mother, do we have our candles ready?
MOTHER:	Yes, tonight we'll light them.
FATHER:	That will guide Lakshmi to our home.
AJAY:	And remind us of how Lord Rama overcame evil.
SHANTI:	Ajay, do you want to help me draw a *rangoli* on the ground in front of our door?
	[pronounced ran-GO-lee]
AJAY:	Yes! Let's make a drawing to welcome Lakshmi.
MOTHER:	I bought some colored chalk for you to use.
SHANTI:	It will be so beautiful.
FATHER:	Just like Lakshmi and Sita.
AJAY:	Happy Divali!
	[Shanti, Father, and Mother]: Happy Divali!
NARRATOR 1:	Divali is celebrated all over the world by Hindus.
NARRATOR 2:	In some places it is celebrated for many days.
NARRATOR 1:	In some places, the celebration focuses on Lord Rama.
NARRATOR 2:	In some places the celebration focuses on Hindu gods and goddesses.
NARRATOR 1:	But everywhere it is celebrated as a festival of lights. . .
NARRATOR 2:	. . . and hope, peace, and a time of new beginnings.

FOLLOW-UP ACTIVITIES

Where in the World Am I? (Geography)

Find India on a world map. Locate the major rivers, mountains, and cities in India; find the longitudinal and latitudinal boundaries of modern-day India.

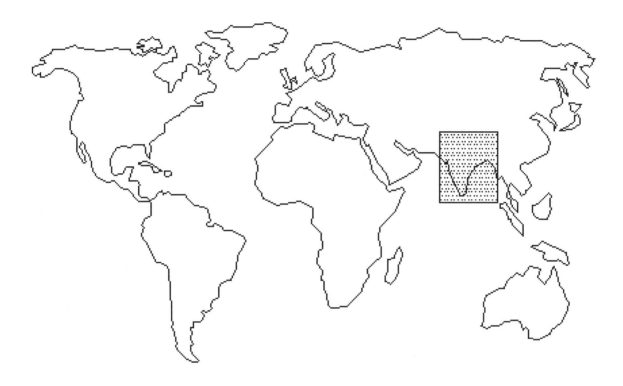

Make a Flag of India (Math, Art)

The flag of India is tricolored. In the center is a wheel called the Dharma Chakra [pronounced DAR-mah SHAH-krah]. The wheel represents progress. The 24 spokes on the wheel represent 24 hours in a day. To make a flag of India, you will need:

❖ Sheet of 9-inch by 12-inch orange construction paper

❖ Sheet of 9-inch by 12-inch green construction paper

❖ Sheet of 9-inch by 12-inch white construction paper

❖ Circle pattern approximately 3 inches in diameter OR a compass

❖ Ruler

❖ Pencil

❖ Blue felt pen

❖ Scissors

❖ Glue

Using a ruler, pencil, and scissors, measure, mark, and cut the white paper to a size 8 inches by 12 inches. Then measure, mark, and cut the orange and green papers into equal strips measuring 2½ inches by 12 inches each. NOTE: These may be cut ahead of time using a paper cutter—or students may work in pairs, measuring, cutting, and sharing the paper as a math tie-in. One strip of orange and one strip of green paper are needed per flag.

Glue one strip of orange paper lengthwise to the top of the white paper, matching top and side edges. Glue one strip of green paper lengthwise to the bottom of the white paper, matching bottom and side edges.

Using the ruler and pencil, locate and mark the center of the white section of paper. Trace around a 3-inch diameter circle centered on that mark, or use a compass and pencil to draw a 3-inch circle with the compass point at the center mark. Go over the circle with a blue felt pen. Then, using the ruler and felt pen, draw 24 spokes from the center to the circle, as shown.

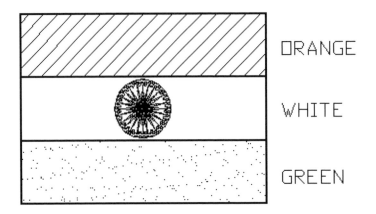

Discuss the math involved in this activity—division of paper into thirds and diameter of a circle. Introduce the geometry of radius, area, and circumference and the number of degrees around the circle for each of the 24 spokes (360 divided by 24). NOTE: The stripes will be approximate in relation to the official ratio. For an additional math activity, recalculate the size of the flag and measurements for the stripes based on the true ratio for a larger size and a smaller size flag.

National Anthem of India (Literacy, Geography, Music)

The national anthem of India is called "Thou Art the Ruler of the Minds of All People, Dispenser of India's Destiny." In the song there are references to many locations in India. As you read through the lyrics, locate as many of the places on a map as you can. Check the library or look online for a recording of the Indian National Anthem.

Glory to thee, ruler of our hearts and of India's destiny!
Punjab, Sind, Gujrat, Maharashtra,
The land of the Dravids, Orissa, Bengal,
The Vindhyas and Himalayas, the Jumuna
And the Ganges and the ceaseless waves of the Ocean
All arise at thy fair name and seek thy blessings,
Singing their hymn of praise to thee.
Glory to thee, Oh Goddess of India's fortune!
Hail, hail, hail to thee forever!

Currency Conversion (Math)

The currency used in India is the rupee [pronounced roo-PEE]. Check an online currency converter or the financial section of a newspaper and compare one rupee with one US dollar. Calculate how much it would cost in rupees to buy:

❖ A candy bar (at US $.50)

❖ A pizza (at US $10.00)

❖ A car (at US $15,000.00)

HAVE A DIVALI CELEBRATION

Make a Divali Lamp (Art)

Make a Divali lamp (called a *diya*). Traditionally, a diya is filled with oil and wicks, but we can use tea lights. To make a diya, you will need:

❖ Self-hardening clay (a ball approximately 2 inches in diameter)

❖ Jar top, cup, or round cookie cutter (approximately 4 inches in diameter)

❖ Plastic knife

❖ Rolling pin or wooden dowel, approximately 6 to 8 inches in length

❖ Tea light candle

Using the rolling pin or dowel, roll the clay to a thickness of about one-half inch. Use a jar top, cup, or cookie cutter as a template (and knife, if needed) to cut a circle from the clay. Turn the edges of the circle up to form a shallow bowl with a flat bottom. Let the clay harden and set the candle in the center.

Saris and Turbans (Costumes, Social Studies)

Different regions and religious groups in India wear different types of traditional clothing. Many women in India wear a sari [pronounced SAH-ree]. Indian men of the Sikh [pronounced SEEK] religion cover their head with a turban. In this activity, girls learn to tie a sari and boys learn to tie one form of turban. The saris and turbans can be used as costumes for the play, or the classroom can use a single length of fabric to experiment with this tying activity. NOTE: If there is concern about hygiene, consider having one narrow length of cloth per child   or choose one girl and one boy to serve as models. Forty-five or sixty-inch-wide fabric can be cut lengthwise to make two saris, or one sari and two turbans.

How to tie a sari

A traditional sari is a long cloth worn over a short-sleeved shirt and a long skirt with a firm, elastic waistband. For this activity, the sari can be worn over street clothes. Use a piece of fabric approximately 3 yards long and 30 inches wide.

First, wrap the fabric around your waist, starting at the left side, going behind your back, wrapping around the right front, and returning to the left side (see first, second, and third illustrations).

Holding the loose fabric on your left side with your left hand, tuck the top edge firmly into the waistband to form a skirt. Allow enough fabric to be able to move your legs.

On the right side of your body fold a section of the loose fabric into 5 to 7 pleats as you would fold a paper fan, but leave the remainder of the length of fabric hanging (you may toss it over your arm or shoulder while making the pleats). With the points of the pleats facing left, tuck them firmly into the waistband (see fourth illustration).

Take the remainder of the fabric and wrap it once more around your waist, back to the front, ending with the loose end in front at your right side

Finally, drape the fabric up over your left shoulder so it hangs down your back behind your left shoulder (see final illustration).

How to tie a turban

The size, color and fabric of turbans differ according to regions and individual preferences. Here is one way to tie a turban.

First, hold one end of cloth (about 8 inches wide) against your left cheek. Take the remaining cloth behind the left side of your head and up behind your head on the right side (see first illustration).

Next, take the cloth down the left front side of your head (left forehead), down behind your head, over to the right side of your neck and back up behind your head (see second illustration).

Next, take the cloth back across your forehead again and over to the back left side of your head. This time, wrap the cloth higher up onto the top of your head to cover any part missed the first time. Bring the cloth back around the back of your head to your right side (see third illustration).

The left side of your head should now be completely covered. Take the cloth up over the head high enough to cover the top of your head and your upper right side and down again. Wrap the material around to the left side, going in the opposite direction and lower than the last wrap to cover more of your head on the right side (see fourth illustration).

Make another lower wrap on the right side, leaving leftover material toward the back of your head. Tuck all leftover material into a crease of the turban at the back of the head. Also tuck the material you held next to your cheek into the turban (see final illustration).

Rangoli (Art, Social Studies)

Rangoli are patterns drawn on the ground near doorways to welcome the goddess Lakshmi. Patterns of animals, trees, symbols, or geometric designs are typically created using colored sand, rice, powder, or chalk. For this activity, use sidewalk chalk. Outside on the cement or blacktop, allow each student an area to design a rangoli. Have each student explain his or her rangoli. Discuss the similarity of this art form to Navajo sand paintings.

Pachisi Game (Math)

The board game of Pachisi [pronounced pah-CHEESE-ee] has been played in India since the fourth century AD. The game board can be photocopied to use in class. Allow one game board for every 2 to 4 students.

Each player should have 4 game pieces of one color. Each player uses a different color—for example, one player would have 4 yellow slips of paper; another player would have 4 green ones. The object of the game is for a player to move all 4 game pieces from the starting point, go around the board, and get back to his home base. The first player to bring all 4 pieces home is the winner.

Each player rolls one die to see who goes first. The player with the lowest roll goes first. Ties are broken with a second roll.

A player must throw a five either on one die or on both dice to bring a game piece into play. When a player rolls a five, he moves his piece into his entry space where indicated. After the player moves his piece, his turn is over—unless he has rolled a double, which gains him another turn. Once a turn is over, it is the turn of the next player to the left.

Once a game piece is in play, roll again to move it around the board the number of spaces on the dice. If a player chooses not to move his piece, he says "pass," and it becomes the next player's turn.

If a roll of the dice lands one player's game piece on a space occupied by another player's game piece, the other player's piece is bumped back to its starting area—unless the space is a "safety space" (marked with a circle on the board).

Two pieces OF THE SAME COLOR may occupy the same space. If they do they become a blockade, and no pieces can move past them—not even pieces of the same color as the blocking pieces. No more than two pieces can occupy a space at the same time.

The middle row of squares in your area is the row used to go home. The exact number on the dice must be rolled to enter the home triangle.

You may bypass your home stretch and make another circle around the board, if you wish to try to bump another player and prevent him from winning.

Discuss counting, strategy, and things that could be used instead of dice to play the game (spinners with numbers, pennies, rocks, etc.).

Barfi Candy Recipe (Math)

Barfi candy is one of the most popular foods at Hindu festivals. It is often given to friends as gifts. To make approximately 20 pieces of barfi candy you will need:

- ❖ 1 cup sugar
- ❖ 1 three-ounce box of vanilla pudding (NOT instant)
- ❖ Bowl
- ❖ Electric skillet
- ❖ 1 can condensed milk
- ❖ 1 cup crushed pistachio nuts
- ❖ ¼ teaspoon ground nutmeg
- ❖ 1 teaspoon cardamom
- ❖ 1 cup grated coconut
- ❖ Large rectangular cake pan, greased

Wash hands before cooking. Mix the dry pudding and condensed milk together until the mixture is crumbly. Add nuts, coconut, and spices. Heat the water and sugar together on low heat, stirring until it becomes a thin syrup. Stir the pudding mixture into the syrup and spread it out in a greased cake pan. The mixture should be approximately 1½ inches deep in the pan. Cool and refrigerate to set, about 4 hours. Cut into squares and serve as candy.

SUGGESTIONS FOR FURTHER ACTIVITIES

History: Research the history of India, including its relationship with Great Britain.

Social Studies: Research customs and beliefs regarding Divali. How is this holiday similar to other holidays students know—and how is it different?

Literacy/Language Arts: Find and read some of the myths about gods and goddesses from Indian culture.

Language Arts: Have students write a poem or story about Divali, including what it means or how it is similar to (or different from) a holiday they celebrate.

Science: Discuss a lunar month and how it relates to a month of our calendar. (See the chapter entitled **Calendars.**)

Science: The elephant is important in much of Indian art and literature. Research the differences and similarities between Indian and African elephants, including their appearance, diet, and natural habitat.

Math: When making barfi, discuss measurement conversions and practice converting fractions and whole numbers and ounces and metric system measurements, using the recipe as a guide. (See the chapter entitled **Measurements and Metric Conversions.**)

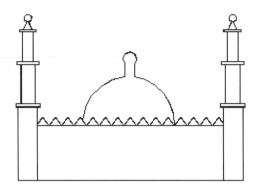

November—Ramadan

(Saudi Arabia, Kuwait)

BACKGROUND

Ramadan [pronounced RAH-mah-dahn] is the ninth month of the Islamic lunar calendar. The people of the Islamic faith believe that in this month, in the year AD 610, their Prophet Muhammad received the words of the Qur'an (the book of Islamic faith) from the Angel Gabriel. To honor this revelation, the people of the Islamic faith fast during the month of Ramadan from sunrise to sunset. At the end of the month, they celebrate *Eid ul-Fitr,* which means "the festival of the breaking of the fast."

READERS THEATRE SCRIPT—THE FIVE PILLARS

Suggested Costumes and Props

- ❖ Small rugs
- ❖ Table
- ❖ Chairs
- ❖ Pillows and blankets (Scene 1)
- ❖ Book (Scene 1)

Characters

The following is a list of characters. Because there are so few roles, consider having different narrators for each of the scenes.

- NARRATOR 1
- NARRATOR 2
- HASSAN

- ADIRA
- AUNT YASMIN
- UNCLE BASHIR

Presentation Suggestions

This play includes 5 scenes. Narrator 1 and Narrator 2 will be onstage at all times. Decorate the back of the stage with flags of Kuwait made by students. The **SETTING** at the beginning of each scene is to assist the characters and is not intended to be read. Performance suggestions (gestures, movements, facial expressions) and pronunciation helps are included in brackets.

The Five Pillars

Scene 1—The First Morning of Ramadan

SETTING: Present day, at the home of a Muslim family. Onstage are Narrator 1, Narrator 2, Aunt Yasmin and Uncle Bashir, and their nephew Hassan and niece Adira, who are visiting them during Ramadan. [names are pronounced yas-MEEN; bah-SHEER; hah-SAHN; ah-DEER-ah]

NARRATOR 1:	The time is the present.
NARRATOR 2:	It is the morning of the first day of Ramadan.
NARRATOR 1:	The setting is the home of a Muslim family.
NARRATOR 2:	Hassan and his sister, Adira, are visiting their Aunt Yasmin and Uncle Bashir.
AUNT YASMIN:	Good morning!
UNCLE BASHIR:	Time to get up.
ADIRA:	It's so early.
HASSAN:	It's still dark outside.
AUNT YASMIN:	Yes, it IS still dark.
UNCLE BASHIR:	So you'd better get up quick.
HASSAN:	Why so early?
UNCLE BASHIR:	You have to get up now if you want to have breakfast.
HASSAN:	Can't we have breakfast later?
AUNT YASMIN:	If you don't eat before sunrise…
UNCLE BASHIR:	…you won't get anything to eat for the rest of the day
ADIRA:	For the rest of the day?
AUNT YASMIN:	Until after sunset.
HASSAN:	Do you mean today is…
AUNT YASMIN:	Yes—today is the first day of Ramadan!
UNCLE BASHIR:	*Eid* greetings!

HASSAN and ADIRA [together]:	Holiday greetings to you, too.
ADIRA:	I know that Ramadan is a holy month, but why is it holy?
UNCLE BASHIR:	It's when the Angel Gabriel came to the Prophet Muhammad. . .
AUNT YASMIN:	. . . and revealed God's word to him.
HASSAN:	Why do we celebrate for a whole month?
UNCLE BASHIR:	It took a month to reveal God's word to Muhammad.
HASSAN:	Tell us about Muhammad.
AUNT YASMIN:	Muhammad was born in Mecca.
HASSAN:	When?
UNCLE BASHIR:	On the western calendar it was in AD 570.
ADIRA:	Where is Mecca?
AUNT YASMIN:	It's a city in the country we know as Saudi Arabia.
HASSAN:	I have my geography book, Uncle Bashir.
ADIRA:	Will you show us where Mecca is?
UNCLE BASHIR:	[pointing to the page of a book] Here is the country of Saudi Arabia.
HASSAN:	Way over to the right of Africa.
ADIRA:	That's really far away from here.
HASSAN:	Tell us more about Muhammad.
AUNT YASMIN:	When he was 40 years old, Muhammad saw a vision of the Angel Gabriel.
UNCLE BASHIR:	Gabriel told Muhammad to teach the world that there is only one God.
HASSAN:	We call God "Allah," right?
AUNT YASMIN:	Yes, Allah.
ADIRA:	And did Muhammad teach the world?
UNCLE BASHIR:	Yes, and Muhammad's followers wrote down his words, which became a book called the Qur'an.
HASSAN:	Our holy book?
AUNT YASMIN:	Yes, our holy book.
ADIRA:	So we celebrate the month when Muhammad received God's word.
HASSAN:	That's a good reason to celebrate.
UNCLE BASHIR:	It's the very best reason to celebrate!

Scene 2—Pillar 1 and Pillar 2

SETTING: A few minutes later. Onstage are Narrator 1, Narrator 2, Hassan, Adira, Aunt Yasmin, and Uncle Bashir.

NARRATOR 1:	Hassan and Adira follow Aunt Yasmin and Uncle Bashir into the living room.
NARRATOR 2:	They are ready to start the day.
UNCLE BASHIR:	First thing we do in the morning is say our morning prayer.
AUNT YASMIN:	As we face the holy city of Mecca.
HASSAN:	But we're visiting you from out of town.
ADIRA:	We don't know which direction Mecca is from here.
UNCLE BASHIR:	Mecca is southeast from us here in America.
AUNT YASMIN:	[pointing] So it's in that direction.
UNCLE BASHIR:	Let's kneel down and bow.
AUNT YASMIN:	And say our declaration of faith.
NARRATOR 1:	Uncle Bashir, Aunt Yasmin, Hassan, and Adira recite together, "There is no god but God. Muhammad is God's messenger."
NARRATOR 2:	Then they pray.
	[A moment of silence, and then Uncle Bashir, Aunt Yasmin, Hassan, and Adira stand]
HASSAN:	Why do we always start our prayers the same way?
ADIRA:	With our declaration of faith?
UNCLE BASHIR:	Our declaration is one of the five pillars of our faith.
ADIRA:	Why is it called a pillar?
HASSAN:	Isn't a pillar like a column in a building?
AUNT YASMIN:	Yes, a pillar holds up the whole building.
UNCLE BASHIR:	The five pillars of Islam are like pillars of a building.
AUNT YASMIN:	Because they hold up our faith.
HASSAN:	So our declaration of faith is the first pillar.
ADIRA:	What's the second?
AUNT YASMIN:	You already did it this morning, too.
ADIRA:	Prayer?
UNCLE BASHIR:	Yes, prayer.

HASSAN:	But we also pray later, too.
ADIRA:	Are all our prayers different pillars?
AUNT YASMIN:	No. All prayers are part of the same pillar.
UNCLE BASHIR:	We pray before sunrise.
ADIRA:	We already did that.
AUNT YASMIN:	What other times do we pray?
HASSAN:	After midday, late afternoon…
ADIRA:	…after sunset, and before midnight.
HASSAN:	So prayer is all one pillar?
UNCLE BASHIR:	Yes.
HASSAN:	It's still dark outside.
ADIRA:	Do we still have time for breakfast?
UNCLE BASHIR:	Yes, the sun hasn't risen yet.
AUNT YASMIN:	Let's eat!

Scene 3—Pillars 3 and 4

SETTING: Breakfast that day. Onstage are Narrator 1, Narrator 2, Hassan, Adira, Aunt Yasmin, and Uncle Bashir.

NARRATOR 1:	Now that morning prayers are over, Hassan, Adira, Aunt Yasmin, and Uncle Bashir go to the kitchen.
NARRATOR 2:	It's time for breakfast.
ADIRA:	I'm so hungry!
HASSAN:	How will we make it all day without eating?
AUNT YASMIN:	Eat plenty now.
ADIRA:	But I'll be hungry later.
UNCLE BASHIR:	It's good to be hungry later.
HASSAN:	How can being hungry be good?
AUNT YASMIN:	Hunger reminds you of all the good things God has given you.
AIDRA:	What do you mean?
UNCLE BASHIR:	When you are hungry you appreciate your food more.

HASSAN:	I'd hate to be hungry my whole life.
AUNT YASMIN:	That's the other reason not to eat during the day.
ADIRA:	What reason is that?
AUNT YASMIN:	The third pillar of Islam.
HASSAN:	What's the third pillar?
UNCLE BASHIR:	We fast to remind ourselves how the poor and hungry people feel.
HASSAN:	But knowing how hungry people feel won't help them.
ADIRA:	We should do something for the poor people.
AUNT YASMIN:	Yes, we should.
UNCLE BASHIR:	Helping people is the fourth pillar of Islam.
HASSAN:	What should we do for the poor?
ADIRA:	Maybe we could give a gift to a family who needs our help.
AUNT YASMIN:	That's a good idea.
ADIRA:	And it'll take our minds off how hungry we are!
HASSAN:	That's a great idea!

Scene 4—Later that Day

SETTING: Evening that day. Present onstage are Narrator 1, Narrator 2, Hassan, Adira, Aunt Yasmin, and Uncle Bashir.

NARRATOR 1:	It is now evening of that same day.
NARRATOR 2:	Hassan, Adira, Aunt Yasmin, and Uncle Bashir are getting ready for dinner.
AUNT YASMIN:	It's almost time for dinner.
HASSAN:	I'm so hungry!
ADIRA:	Me, too!
UNCLE BASHIR:	Did you say your midday prayers?
HASSAN:	Yes, I did.
ADIRA:	Me, too.
AUNT YASMIN:	And your afternoon prayers?
ADIRA:	Yes—those, too!

HASSAN:	Me, too.
UNCLE BASHIR:	Good for you.
ADIRA:	Something smells really good.
HASSAN:	What are you cooking, Aunt Yasmin?
AUNT YASMIN:	Lamb stew.
ADIRA:	Yum!
AUNT YASMIN:	And ma'amoul cookies for dessert.
HASSAN:	Double yum!
UNCLE BASHIR:	But first we pray our after-sunset prayer.
AUNT YASMIN:	Yes. Do you remember which way is Mecca?
HASSAN and ADIRA [Pointing]:	That way!
AUNT YASMIN:	That's right.
UNCLE BASHIR:	Let's kneel, bow toward Mecca, and pray.

Scene 5—The Fifth Pillar

SETTING: At the dinner table. Onstage are Narrator 1, Narrator 2, Hassan, Adira, Uncle Bashir, and Aunt Yasmin.

NARRATOR 1:	It's dinnertime.
HASSAN:	Dinner is great, Aunt Yasmin!
AUNT YASMIN:	Thank you.
ADIRA:	I was so hungry.
UNCLE BASHIR:	How did you feel today, besides hungry?
ADIRA:	I kept thinking about that family we saw.
AUNT YASMIN:	The family that was living in the park.
HASSAN:	I didn't like thinking about not having enough food every day.
ADIRA:	It felt nice shopping for them.
HASSAN:	And then giving the bag of food to them.
ADIRA:	I'll bet they're glad to have a nice dinner tonight, too!
AUNT YASMIN:	I'm sure they are.

[No one speaks for a moment]

UNCLE BASHIR: Why are you two kids so quiet?

ADIRA: We've been thinking all day about something else.

AUNT YASMIN: What is it?

HASSAN: You said there are five pillars of faith.

UNCLE BASHIR: That's right.

ADIRA: It's nighttime now.

HASSAN: We've declared our faith, prayed, fasted, and given to the poor.

AUNT YASMIN: Yes, we have.

UNCLE BASHIR: So what are you wondering?

ADIRA: We are wondering what's left.

AUNT YASMIN: What do you mean "what's left"?

HASSAN: Declaring, praying, fasting, and giving are only four pillars.

ADIRA: What's the fifth pillar of faith?

AUNT YASMIN: The last pillar is a special one.

UNCLE BASHIR: It's not one you do every day, or even every year.

HASSAN: What is it?

AUNT YASMIN: The fifth pillar of faith is called the *hajj*.

[pronounced HAHJ]

ADIRA: The hajj?

HASSAN: What does that mean?

UNCLE BASHIR: The fifth pillar of faith says that every Muslim should travel to the holy city at least once in their life.

ADIRA: To Mecca?

AUNT YASMIN: Yes, to Mecca.

HASSAN: But that's across the world from here.

UNCLE BASHIR: Yes, it's a very long trip.

AUNT YASMIN: But making the effort shows how important your faith is to you.

HASSAN: I'd like to go to Mecca.

UNCLE BASHIR: So would I.

ADIRA: You've never been to Mecca either, Uncle Bashir?

UNCLE BASHIR: Not yet.

AUNT YASMIN: Neither have I.

HASSAN:	Why not?
AUNT YASMIN:	We were waiting to go with someone special.
ADIRA:	Special how?
UNCLE BASHIR:	Special like you two.
HASSAN:	Like us?
AUNT YASMIN:	Yes. You are our favorite niece and nephew.
ADIRA:	Aunt Yasmin, we're your ONLY niece and nephew.
AUNT YASMIN:	That makes you extra special!
UNCLE BASHIR:	So what do you think, kids?
AUNT YASMIN:	Shall we ask your parents if we can plan a trip to Mecca?
ADIRA:	You mean we could go now?
UNCLE BASHIR:	We were thinking about next year during Ramadan.
AUNT YASMIN:	I'll get the calendar.
ADIRA:	I'll get some paper.
HASSAN:	I'll get my map.
UNCLE BASHIR:	I'll get the phone.
HASSAN:	This will be awesome!
ADIRA:	Happy Ramadan, Aunt Yasmin and Uncle Bashir!
AUNT YASMIN and UNCLE BASHIR:	Eid greetings!

FOLLOW-UP ACTIVITIES

Where in the World Am I? (Geography)

Find the area of the Middle East on a world map. Locate the countries of Kuwait, Saudi Arabia, Iran, Iraq, Pakistan, and Egypt, which are some of the countries where people celebrate Ramadan. Discuss other places around the world where people of the Islamic faith live. Locate the major rivers, mountains, and cities in the Arab countries and find their longitudinal and latitudinal boundaries.

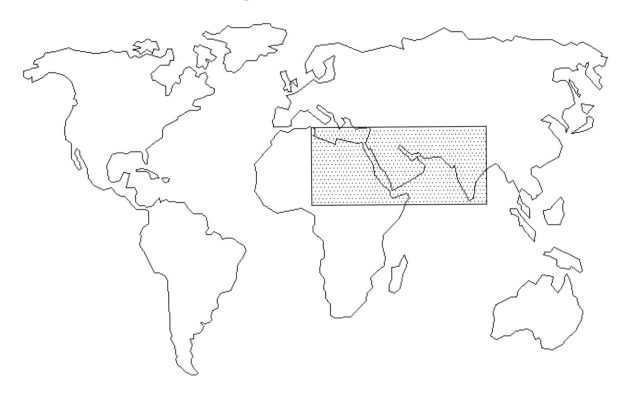

Make a Flag of Kuwait (Math, Art)

The flag of Kuwait is representative of many of the flags of Arab countries. Many countries show unity with other Arab countries by using the pan-Arabian colors of green, red, white, and black. Red often represents courage, revolution, hardiness, blood, and valor. White often represents peace. Black often represents determination. Green symbolizes the Muslim religion. Many Arab flags are also longer and narrower than flags of western countries. The Kuwaiti flag has a ratio of 1:2 (width to length). To make a flag of Kuwait you will need:

❖ Sheet of 9-inch by-12 inch green construction paper

❖ Sheet of 9-inch by 12-inch red construction paper

❖ Sheet of 9-inch by 12-inch white construction paper

❖ Sheet of 9-inch by 12-inch black construction paper

❖ Scissors

❖ Ruler

❖ Pencil

❖ Glue

❖ Protractor

Using a ruler, pencil, and scissors, measure, mark, and cut the white sheet of paper to a size 6 inches by 12 inches. Measure, mark, and cut each of the green and red sheets of paper into strips 2 inches wide and 12 inches long. Measure, mark, and cut the black paper into a piece 3 inches wide and 6 inches long. NOTE: You may cut the paper ahead of time using a paper cutter. Each sheet of colored construction paper will make more than one flag. However, to use this as a math activity, have students measure and cut the paper while working in groups—one student measuring and cutting the green paper; one the red; and one the black.

Place the 3-inch by 6-inch black paper in front of you vertically. Measure and mark 2 inches down from the top right corner and 2 inches up from the bottom right corner. Using the ruler and pencil, draw a line from the top left corner to the top right mark. Draw a line from the bottom left corner to the bottom right mark. Cut along the lines, to leave an isosceles trapezoid. The left (long) side of the trapezoid should measure 6 inches. The right (short) side of the trapezoid should measure 3 inches.

Lay the white paper in front of you horizontally. Glue the green strip horizontally to the white paper, matching the top edges. Glue the red strip horizontally to the white paper, matching the bottom edges. Finally, glue the black trapezoid to the left side of the flag, over the green, white, and red paper, matching the long edge of the trapezoid with the left edge of the white paper.

Using a protractor, measure the angles of the isosceles trapezoid. What are the angles for each of the corners? Discuss the flag's ratio, angles, and geometric shapes used (rectangle, trapezoid). Recalculate the measurements for a larger size and smaller size flag as an additional math activity.

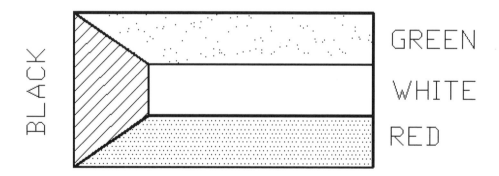

National Anthem of Kuwait (Literacy, Music)

Following are the first two stanzas of the Kuwaiti National Anthem. Check the library or look online for a recording of the music.

Kuwait, Kuwait, Kuwait,
My country,
In peace live, in dignity,
Your face bright,
Your face bright,
Your face bright with majesty,
Kuwait, Kuwait, Kuwait,
My country.

Oh cradle of ancestry,
Who put down its memory,
With everlasting symmetry,
Showing all eternity,
Those Arabs were Heavenly,
Kuwait, Kuwait, Kuwait,
My country.

Currency Conversion (Math)

The currency used in Kuwait is the dinar [pronounced dih-NAR]. Check an online currency converter or the financial section of a newspaper and compare one dinar with one US dollar. Calculate how many dinar it would cost to buy:

❖ A candy bar (at US $.50)

❖ A pizza (at US $10.00)

❖ A car (at US $15,000.00)

HAVE A RAMADAN CELEBRATION

Ma'amoul Cookie Recipe (Math)

Snack on dates and water, pistachio nuts, sugared almonds, apricot juice, dried fruit, and ma'amoul cookies, which are part of a traditional Ramadan feast. Double or triple the recipe for a math curriculum tie-in. To make one dozen cookies, you will need:

❖ 2 pounds finely chopped dates

❖ ¼ pound soft butter

❖ 1 pound melted butter

❖ 1 cup chopped walnuts

❖ 1½ pounds semolina flour (from a Middle Eastern grocery store)

❖ 1 cup sugar

* ❖ 3 tablespoons hot water

* ❖ 2 or 3 tablespoons powdered sugar for dusting

* ❖ Measuring cup

* ❖ Measuring spoons

* ❖ 1 small bowl

* ❖ 1 medium bowl

* ❖ 1 large bowl with cover (may use plastic wrap)

* ❖ Fork

* ❖ Baking sheet

Wash hands before cooking. In a small bowl, microwave a pound of butter until melted. In a medium bowl, mix the chopped dates, walnuts, and the remaining ¼ pound of butter with a fork. In large bowl, mix the flour and sugar until blended. Add the melted butter to the flour mixture a little bit at a time. Mix together with hands. Cover bowl for 1 hour.

Preheat oven to 450. Add 2 to 3 tablespoons of hot water to the dough, a little at a time, to soften it, mixing with hands. Roll the dough into 12 balls. Flatten each ball into a circle about 4 inches in diameter and place on an ungreased baking sheet. Place about 1 tablespoon of the date and nut mixture in the center of each dough circle. Pull the edges of the cookie up over the top of the filling and press together to seal. Use a fork to press a design on top of the cookie.

Bake for 20 minutes until golden brown. When slightly cool, sprinkle with powdered sugar.

Eid Greeting Cards (Language Arts, Art)

It is typical for Muslims to send greeting cards to one another during Ramadan. Create Eid greeting cards, with Arabic designs or a mosque shape. To make the greeting cards you will need:

* ❖ Construction paper (any color)—a half sheet (4½ by 12 inches) for each card

* ❖ Colored marking pens

* ❖ Pencils

* ❖ Scissors

* ❖ Glue

* ❖ Glitter, ribbons, other optional decorations

Fold a piece of paper in half to create a 4½- by 6-inch card. On the outside, draw a design or cut out a mosque shape and glue it to the front, using the designs provided here for inspiration. On the inside, write "Eid Greetings."

While making greeting cards, introduce and discuss the terms *Islam,* which means "submission to the will of God" and *Muslim,* which means "one who submits."

Helping the Community (Physical Education, Community Service)

Organize a class project to help the community or school. Ideas might include:

❖ Have a bake sale. Sell ma'amoul cookies to raise money for a needy family or school improvement.

❖ Spend time at recess, break, or after school picking up trash, sweeping, or cleaning up the classroom or school.

❖ Walk along the streets or around the school picking up trash.

❖ Plant flowers in front of your school or city park.

❖ Make cards or decorations to take to the local hospital or retirement home.

❖ Think up your own ideas to make your community better.

Muslim Calendar (Math, Science, Literacy, Language Arts, Art)

The Muslim lunar calendar is based on the moon's appearance in the sky. A lunar year is generally 11 days shorter than a solar year. Because the Muslim calendar is not in line with our solar calendar, students will not be able to easily create an accurate Muslim calendar. Instead, use a western calendar to copy the number of days in each month. Then use the Muslim names for the days of the week and rename the twelve months, using the Muslim months. Students may decorate their calendars, if desired.

NOTE: This activity is *not* intended to recreate an accurate Muslim calendar. Rather, it is intended as a math/science activity to introduce students to differences in our calendars and as a literacy/language arts introduction to certain Muslim words.

The following are the days of the week and the 12 lunar months of the Muslim calendar:

Month	Name of Month
1	Muharram
2	Safar
3	Rabi' l
4	Rabi' ll
5	Jumada l
6	Jumada ll
7	Rajab
8	Sha'ban
9	Ramadan
10	Shawwal
11	Dhu-l-Qa'da
12	Dhu-l-Hijja

The days of the week in a Muslim calendar follow the order of our calendar, beginning with Sunday and ending with Saturday.

Our Day of the Week	Muslim Name
Sunday	yaum al-ahad
Monday	yaum al-itsnayna
Tuesday	yaum ats-tsalatsa
Wednesday	yaum al-arba a
Thursday	yaum al-khomis
Friday	yaum al-jum a
Saturday	yaum as-sabt

In the western calendar, we date history back in time to the birth of Christ. (See the chapter entitled **Calendars.**) The Muslim calendar counts from the prophet Muhammad's flight (called the Hirjah) from Mecca to Medina. The initials **AH** stand for the Latin phrase *anno Hegirae* and refer to the years after Muhammad's flight. A year designated **H** is some year before that date.

On our solar calendar, the year of Muhammad's Hirjah was our year AD 622. But because the Muslim lunar year is not the same length as our solar year, we cannot use simple mathematics to compare dates. For example, if the Hirjah was AD 622, we cannot then say that all dates in the Muslim calendar can be calculated by subtracting 622 years from our present year. For a very rough estimate, though, we can compare Muslim years and our years by multiplying the Islamic year number by .97 and adding 622 to that figure. Try using that equation to determine dates between the two calendars.

Locating Mecca (Geography, Science)

The Islamic faith requires Muslims to turn toward their holy city of Mecca to pray. No matter where they are in the world, they need to know the direction of Mecca. This science activity will help students learn about geographical location and compass direction, as well as understand the sun's path across our sky.

Mecca is located in the modern country of Saudi Arabia. From anywhere in the continental United States, the direction to Mecca is southeast. (Mecca may be slightly north and east from some places in Hawaii.) On a sunny day, have students shove a stick (such as a chopstick or a pencil) into the ground outside. With a small rock, mark the shadow made on the ground.

If this activity is done in the morning, the shadow should be on the west side of the stick. If done in the afternoon, the shadow should be on the east side of the stick. Return every hour to mark the new shadow with a different rock. The rocks will give students a visual representation of the sun's path across the sky from east to west. With that information, discuss how to locate southeast.

For an expanded science tie-in, use a magnetic compass to locate the direction of Mecca. Discuss how a compass works with the earth's magnetic north. Include a discussion of the earth's magnetic north versus true north.

SUGGESTIONS FOR FURTHER ACTIVITIES

History: Research the life of the Prophet Muhammad.

Social Studies: Research and compare flags of various Arab countries. How are they similar? How are they different?

Language Arts: Have students write a poem or story about community, or about doing things for others.

Science: One type of animal that lives in many parts of the Middle East is the camel. Research camels—why do some have one hump and some have two? What is the purpose of the hump? What animal from South America is related to camels, and how?

Math: When making ma'amoul cookies, discuss measurement conversions and practice converting fractions and whole numbers and ounces and metric system measurements, using the recipe as a guide. (See the chapter entitled **Measurements and Metric Conversions.**)

December—Las Posadas

(Mexico)

BACKGROUND

Las Posadas [pronounced LAS poh-SAH-das] is part of the Christian celebration of Christmas. For nine days beginning December 16, people in Mexico reenact the journey of Mary and Joseph (the mother and stepfather of Jesus Christ) to Bethlehem. This reenactment began in the sixteenth century.

READERS THEATRE SCRIPT—OUTSIDE THE INN

Suggested Costumes and Props

- ❖ Farole—paper lantern attached to long pole (Scenes 4 and 5)
- ❖ Unlit candles (Scenes 4 and 5)
- ❖ Baseball bat (Scene 6)
- ❖ Blindfold (Scene 6)
- ❖ Tunic for Mary, angel, Joseph, shepherd—others in the parade, as desired (Scenes 4, 5, and 6)
- ❖ Halo for the angel—yellow paper or tinfoil (Scenes 4, 5, and 6)
- ❖ Broom with bristles covered with paper and decorated as a burro's face (Scenes 4 and 5)

199

Characters

The following is a list of characters. Different students can take the parts of Narrator 1 and Narrator 2 for each scene, to allow opportunities for more students to participate.

- NARRATOR 1
- NARRATOR 2
- ROSA
- JOSE
- MAMA HERNANDEZ

- ROBERTO
- FELICIA
- PAPA RAMIREZ
- MRS. GARCIA
- MR. GARCIA

Presentation Suggestions

This play includes 6 scenes. Narrator 1 and Narrator 2 will be onstage at all times. Consider decorating the back of the stage area with Mexican flags made by students. The **SETTING** at the beginning of each scene is to assist the characters and is not intended to be read. Performance suggestions (gestures, movements, facial expressions) and pronunciation helps are included in brackets.

Outside the Inn

Scene 1—At the Hernandez Home

SETTING: Present day—December 19, at the home of the Hernandez family. Onstage are Narrator 1, Narrator 2, Jose, Mama Hernandez, and Rosa.

NARRATOR 1:	In Mexico, people celebrate Christmas with Las Posadas.
NARRATOR 2:	Las Posadas means "the inns."
NARRATOR 1:	It reenacts the journey that Mary and Joseph took to Bethlehem.
NARRATOR 2:	Where Jesus—who Christians believe is the Son of God—was born.
NARRATOR 1:	For nine evenings, families have parades to different homes.
NARRATOR 2:	In some parades, people hold figures of Mary and Joseph.
NARRATOR 1:	In other parades, children play the roles of Mary and Joseph.
NARRATOR 2:	Let's see what's happening at the Hernandez home.
JOSE:	Mama, it's not fair!
MAMA:	What's not fair, Jose?
JOSE:	Why do girls always get to ride the burro in Las Posadas? Chico is MY burro!
MAMA:	Girls ride the burro because it was Mary who rode it on the first Christmas. Would you like to play the part of Mary?
JOSE:	Pretend to be a girl? No way!
MAMA:	Then be happy you're going to be a shepherd.
JOSE:	It's not a very important part.
MAMA:	The shepherds were the first ones to visit Baby Jesus.
JOSE:	The first? Well, maybe being a shepherd could be okay.
	[Jose exits and Rosa enters]
ROSA:	Mama, I don't want to play the part of Mary.

From *Around the World Through Holidays: Cross Curricular Readers Theatre* written and illustrated by Carol Peterson. Westport, CT: Teacher Ideas Press/Libraries Unlimited. Copyright © 2006.

MAMA:	Why not, Rosa? Mary is the one who gets to ride the burro.
ROSA:	Burros! I was just petting Chico and he tried to bite me! Please don't make me ride him.
MAMA:	Playing Mary is one of the most important parts to play in Las Posadas. Mary was the mother of Baby Jesus.
ROSA:	I know. But I'm scared Chico will bite me!
MAMA:	Maybe Chico was just hungry. We'll make sure Jose feeds him before we go.

Scene 2—At the Ramirez Home

SETTING: The same day, at the home of the Ramirez family. Onstage are Narrator 1, Narrator 2, Roberto, Papa Ramirez, and Felicia.

NARRATOR 1:	At the Ramirez house, they are getting ready for Las Posadas, too.
NARRATOR 2:	Roberto is talking to his father.
ROBERTO:	Papa, why do I have to play the part of Joseph this year?
PAPA:	Why wouldn't you want to be Joseph, Roberto?
ROBERTO:	The Hernandez' burro is really stubborn. Last year when the boy who played Joseph was leading him, Chico decided to munch on the Garcias' bushes. What if I can't handle Chico?
PAPA:	You'll do fine. It's an honor to play the part of Joseph. Joseph was a good stepfather to Jesus.
ROBERTO:	I know, but Chico doesn't like me.
PAPA:	Why don't you visit Jose and see if he'll give you some ideas on how to handle Chico.
ROBERTO:	Okay—see you later.
	[Roberto exits and Felicia enters]
PAPA:	Felicia, have you tried on your Las Posadas costume?
FELICIA:	Yes, but the crown keeps slipping off my head.
PAPA:	It's not a crown—it's your halo, my Las Posadas angel!
FELICIA:	I don't want to be an angel. I don't have enough hair to keep the halo on my head.

PAPA:	You make a beautiful angel.
FELICIA:	But I have to carry the *farole* candle. What if my halo slips and I drop the candle?
	[pronounced fah-ROLE]
PAPA:	You worry too much.
FELICIA:	Can I just not carry the candle tonight?
PAPA:	The candle represents the star that guided the wise men to Baby Jesus. We can't have Las Posadas without an angel and her star leading the way.
FELICIA:	Okay. I just wish I could keep the halo on my head. Where did Roberto go?
PAPA:	He went over to see if Jose had any tips on handling Chico.
FELICIA:	Oh, I just love Chico. Last week, he ate hay right out of my hand.
PAPA:	Why don't you help Jose give Roberto some tips on handling Chico?
FELICIA:	Okay, and I'll see if Rosa needs help with her costume.

Scene 3—Some Things to Know

SETTING: No one on stage except for Narrator 1 and Narrator 2.

NARRATOR 1:	Las Posadas is a celebration from Mexico.
NARRATOR 2:	It means "the inns." An inn is like a hotel.
NARRATOR 1:	Las Posadas is a parade to act out the night Jesus was born…
NARRATOR 2:	…When Jesus' mother, Mary, and her husband Joseph traveled to Bethlehem.
NARRATOR 1:	They went to Bethlehem to pay their taxes.
NARRATOR 2:	While they were on the trip, it was time for Jesus to be born.
NARRATOR 1:	There weren't any hospitals then.
NARRATOR 2:	So Mary and Joseph tried to find a room at an inn to have her baby.
NARRATOR 1:	But many other people were in Bethlehem to pay taxes, too.
NARRATOR 2:	All of the inns were filled up.

NARRATOR 1:	Finally one innkeeper told them they could stay in his stable with the animals.
NARRATOR 2:	That's where Jesus was born.
NARRATOR 1:	In Mexico, Las Posadas is often performed every day for the nine days before Christmas.
NARRATOR 2:	The nine days represent the nine months before Jesus was born.

Scene 4—Preparing for the Procession

SETTING: That night in town. Onstage are Narrator 1, Narrator 2, Jose, Rosa, Felicia, Roberto, Mama. Hernandez, Papa Ramirez, and other townspeople and children.

NARRATOR 1:	Later that night the people gather for the Las Posadas parade.
PAPA:	Everyone line up. Rosa—I mean Mary—get on the burro. Roberto, hold Chico steady for her.
MAMA:	Shepherd Jose, why are you scratching?
JOSE:	This costume is itchy. I'm allergic to wool.
PAPA:	Wool comes from sheep. Shepherds aren't supposed to be allergic to wool!
MAMA:	Angel Felicia, put your halo back on your head.
FELICIA:	It keeps falling off.
ROSA:	Ouch! Chico bit me!
ROBERTO:	He won't stay still.
JOSE:	You just need to hold his bridle. . .
FELICIA:	. . .and speak softly.
JOSE, ROSA, ROBERTO, and FELICIA:	I've got an idea!

Scene 5—On to the Garcia Home

SETTING: A little later; the procession has begun. Onstage are Narrator 1, Narrator 2, Jose, Rosa, Felicia, Roberto, Mama Hernandez, Papa Ramirez, and other townspeople and children. Mr. and Mrs. Garcia stand at stage left or right.

FELICIA: I can't believe I get to be Mary in Las Posadas!

ROSA: And I get to lead the procession!

FELICIA: You're a perfect angel, Rosa. Your thick hair keeps the halo on your head.

ROSA: And Chico likes you, Felicia!

FELICIA: I like him, too!

JOSE: Just relax, Chico. Tonight will be fun!

ROBERTO: He sure minds you well, Jose.

JOSE: We're good friends. Hey, Roberto, you look good as a shepherd.

ROBERTO: The shepherds were the first ones to visit Jesus. And besides, Jose, you've got the perfect name to be Joseph!

PAPA: Everyone ready? Let's go.

MAMA: Tonight Las Posadas ends at the Garcia house.

NARRATOR 1:   The group walks through the streets to the Garcia house.

NARRATOR 2:   They sing special songs about Mary, Joseph, and Baby Jesus.

NARRATOR 1:   Everyone carries candles.

NARRATOR 2:   And they use noisemakers to celebrate.

[the group walks around the stage in a procession and then stops]

NARRATOR 1:   When the group reaches the Garcia house they stop and knock on the door.

NARRATOR 2:   They chant or sing special Las Posadas songs.

EVERYONE: [singing or chanting] Who will give lodging to these pilgrims, who arrive exhausted from traveling the roads?

[Rosa pretends to knock on the door]

JOSE: Please may we come in?

MR. GARCIA: We have no rooms. We're all filled up.

[Rosa pretends to knock on the door again]

JOSE:	Please may we come in? My wife is going to have a baby.
MRS. GARCIA:	We have no rooms. We're all filled up.
	[Rosa pretends to knock on the door again]
JOSE:	Please may we come in? My wife is giving birth to the Son of God.
MR. AND MRS. GARCIA:	The Son of God? Come on in!
	[Mr. and Mrs. Garcia open the door and welcome them in]
NARRATOR 1:	Everyone in the Las Posadas parade enters the Garcia house.
NARRATOR 2:	After a prayer, there's a big party.

Scene 6—The Party

SETTING: Later at the Garcia home. Onstage are Narrator 1, Narrator 2, the Las Posadas parade, Mr. and Mrs. Garcia, and other guests.

JOSE:	These are great cookies, Mrs. Garcia.
MRS. GARCIA:	Thank you. I just love cinnamon.
MR. GARCIA:	Who wants more hot chocolate?
ROSA:	I do!
JOSE:	Not me. I'm waiting for the piñata.
ROSA:	You're right. Hot chocolate can wait.
FELICIA:	Let's get in line.
ROBERTO:	I'll get the bat and the blindfold.
NARRATOR 1:	The children line up.
NARRATOR 2:	They take turns being blindfolded and spun in circles, before swinging at a piñata.
NARRATOR 1:	A piñata is like a decorated, fancy-shaped box.
NARRATOR 1:	It hangs from a tree.
NARRATOR 2:	The children try to break it open with a bat.
JOSE:	I love piñatas!
FELICIA:	They're so colorful.
ROSA:	I love hitting them!

ROBERTO: I love the candy inside!

EVERYONE: Me, too!

JOSE: Why is Las Posadas piñata star-shaped? For my birthday I had a piñata in the shape of a car.

FELICIA: Why isn't the piñata shaped like a burro or a sheep? They're part of Las Posadas, too.

ROSA: But the star led the way to Bethlehem.

FELICIA: And we hang the piñata up high—like it's in the sky.

ROBERTO: It'd be silly to hang a sheep in the sky.

JOSE: Or poor Chico!

[Other children in line continue to be blindfolded so they can swing and hit the piñata]

JOSE: Why do they spin us around so many times?

FELICIA: I always lose count.

ROBERTO: I get so dizzy!

ROSA: They spin us 33 times—one time for every year that Jesus lived.

JOSE: It's fun to watch people try and hit the piñata when they're dizzy.

ROSA: Watch out! Maria's got the bat and she's really dizzy!

[Everyone ducks]

NARRATOR 1: Maria swung and hit the piñata.

NARRATOR 2: It broke open, spilling candy all over the ground.

[The children run to collect the candy]

EVERYONE: Goodies! Enough for everyone!

FOLLOW-UP ACTIVITIES

Where in the World Am I? (Geography)

Find Mexico on a world map. Locate the major rivers, mountains, cities, and the longitudinal and latitudinal boundaries of Mexico.

Make a Flag of Mexico (Math, Art)

The Mexican flag is tricolored. The green on the Mexican flag stands for independence; the white for purity of religion; and the red for honor, and for the union of the Americas and the Iberians (people from Spain).

The emblem of the eagle with a serpent in its claws comes from Mexican legend about the founding of an ancient Aztec city on an island. On the island is a cactus. Its red fruit symbolizes the human heart. An oak branch at the bottom left side of the emblem symbolizes strength. A laurel branch at the bottom right side of the emblem symbolizes victory. To make a Mexican flag you will need:

- ❖ 1 photocopy of the Mexican emblem on white paper
- ❖ 1 sheet of 8½-inch by 14-inch white paper
- ❖ Sheet of 9 by 12-inch green construction paper
- ❖ Sheet of 9 by 12-inch red construction paper
- ❖ Ruler
- ❖ Pencil
- ❖ Scissors

❖ Glue

❖ Green, red, blue, orange, and brown markers

Using ruler, pencil, and scissors, measure, mark, and cut the white paper to a size 8 inches by 13½ inches. Then measure, mark, and cut the green and red papers to a size 4½ inches by 8 inches.

NOTE: You will be able to make 2 flags from each set of red and green papers. Paper can be cut ahead of time using a paper cutter, or to use this activity as a math tie-in, two students can work together. One student measures and cuts the green paper, the other student measures and cuts the red paper, and then they share.

Place the white paper horizontally in front of you. Glue the green paper vertically to the left side of the white paper, matching edges. Glue the red paper vertically to the right side of the white paper, matching edges.

Color the photocopied emblem as follows: brown eagle with orange beak and feet; blue water with brown island; green serpent, cactus, and oak and laurel leaves; 3 red flowers on cactus; green, white, and red ribbon at the base, coloring from left to right. Locate a colored picture of the Mexican emblem in the library or online to help students match colors. Cut the emblem out along the circle and glue it in the center of the white section of the flag.

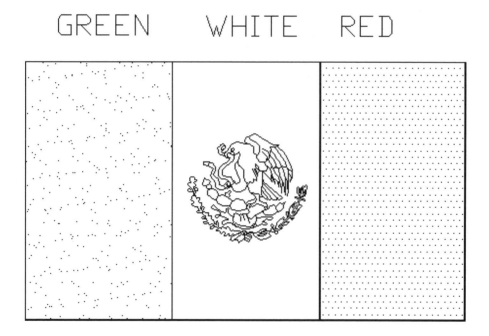

The ratio of the Mexican flag is 4:7 (width to length). Recalculate the dimensions of the flag, using this ratio. What would the size of the flag be if the width were 6 inches? What would the size of the flag be if the length were 20 inches?

National Anthem of Mexico (Literacy, Music)

The following are the words to the Mexican National Anthem. Check the library or look online for a recording.

CHORUS

Mexicans, when the trumpet is calling,
Grasp your sword and your harness assemble.
Let the guns with their thunder appalling
Make the Earth's deep foundations to tremble.
Let the guns with their thunder appalling
Make the Earth's deep foundations to tremble.

May the angel divine,
O dear Homeland,
Crown thy brow with the olive branch of peace;
For thy destiny, traced by God's own hand
In the heavens, shall ever increase
But should ever the proud foe assail thee,
And with insolent foot profane thy ground,
Know, dear Country, thy sons shall not fail thee,
Ev'ry one thy soldier shall be found,
Thy soldier ev'ry one shall be found.

Repeat **CHORUS**

Currency Conversion (Math)

The currency used in Mexico is the peso [pronounced PAY-so]. Check an online currency converter or the financial section of a newspaper and compare one peso with one US dollar. Calculate how much it would cost in pesos to buy:

❖ A candy bar (at US $.50)

❖ A pizza (at US $10.00)

❖ A car (at US $15,000.00)

HAVE A LAS POSADAS CELEBRATION

Bizcochito Recipe (Math)

Snack on bizcochitos [pronounced biz-ko-CHEE-tos]. The ancient Mayan civilization lived in the land that is now Mexico. Ancient Mayans grew cacao [pronounced kah-KAH-oo] beans, from which they made chocolate. Cacao beans were so valuable that they were used by Mayans as money. Enjoy your bizcochitos with a cup of hot chocolate and be grateful to those ancient people living in the land that is now Mexico!

If the classroom has access to an oven, make bizcochitos—cinnamon and anise (licorice) cookies. Or they can be made by one or two students at home to share with the class. Store-bought cinnamon cookies are a quick and easy alternative. To make 48 bizcochito cookies you will need:

❖ 1 cup shortening

❖ ½ cup sugar

❖ 1 egg

❖ 3 cups flour

❖ 1½ teaspoon baking powder

❖ ½ teaspoon salt

❖ 1 teaspoon anise seed

❖ 3 tablespoons water

❖ Additional ¼ cup sugar

❖ 1 tablespoon cinnamon

❖ Large mixing bowl

❖ Small mixing bowl

❖ Measuring cup

❖ Measuring spoons

❖ Electric mixer or wooden spoon

❖ Rolling pin

❖ Extra flour for rolling

❖ Optional star-shaped cookie cutter or knife

❖ Baking sheet

❖ Metal spatula

Wash hands before cooking. Preheat oven to 350. Mix the shortening and ½ cup sugar until creamy. Add the egg and beat. Add flour, baking powder, water, and anise seed. Mix well. Roll out dough on floured surface to ¼ inch thick. Cut into squares or use star-shaped cookie cutter. Mix the remaining sugar and cinnamon together and sprinkle onto each cookie. Bake for 15 to 20 minutes, until light brown.

Faroles and Farolitos (Art)

Faroles are lanterns carried during the Las Posadas procession. Farolitos are "little lanterns," sometimes called luminaries. To make paper faroles to use as props for the play, you will need:

❖ One sheet of white 11- by 17-inch construction paper

❖ Scissors

❖ Glue

❖ Strip of paper approximately 1 inch wide and 6 inches long

Fold the sheet of paper in half lengthwise. Cut from the fold to about 1 inch from the open edge, as shown. Open the paper and roll it horizontally to make a cylinder. Glue the edges together. Glue the strip of paper to the top of the lantern to create a handle.

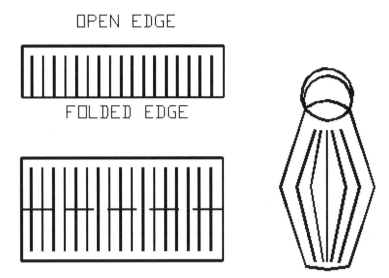

OPEN EDGE

FOLDED EDGE

Farolitos are candles set in bags, which line the roadways during the Las Posadas procession. Students can make them to set across the stage area for the play or to take home and light in front of their house, under adult supervision. To make a farolito you will need:

❖ Lunch-sized paper bag

❖ 2 cups of sand

❖ Votive or tea candle

❖ Scissors

Cut designs in the top half of the paper bag by folding the bag lengthwise and cutting slits or small holes in a design at the top half of the bag only. Place sand in the bag below the level of the holes and secure a votive candle in the sand, allowing space above the sand for the candle to burn.

Piñata (Math, Art)

Make one or more piñatas to use as a prop for the play, to decorate the classroom, and to break open at a Las Posadas party. The piñata will need to dry for at least a day, so plan ahead. To make a piñata you will need:

❖ One large round balloon for each piñata

❖ Papier-mâché (4 cups per bowl)

❖ 2 cups of warm water per bowl

❖ Large bowls or tubs (1 bowl for every 3 to 4 students in the group)

❖ Measuring cup for papier-mâché powder

❖ Separate measuring cup for water

❖ Large mixing spoon

❖ Newspaper—ripped into strips approximately 1 inch by 4 inches

❖ Colored paper—ripped into strips approximately 1inch by 4 inches

❖ 7 sheets of heavy paper for cones

❖ Water, soap, and towels for cleanup

❖ Old shirts or aprons (this can get messy)

❖ Decorations—paint, paintbrushes, colored paper, yarn, glitter, crepe paper strips

❖ Glue

❖ Scissors

❖ Sharp knife to cut hole at top of piñata

❖ Large nail for punching hole in piñata

❖ Wrapped candies or small toys

❖ Bat or long stick to break piñata

❖ Blindfold

❖ Heavy string, wire, or light rope (6 to 8 inches) for hook

❖ Rope for hanging piñata

Consider doing this activity outside. If done indoors, cover tables with newspaper. Mix papier-mâché and water in a large bowl to a thin mixture—allow 3 to 4 students per bowl. Blow up balloon and tie the end. Dip strips of newspaper into papier-mâché. Smooth off excess by running the strip through fingers. Place wet strip onto balloon and smooth down. Overlap strips until balloon is covered by 3 to 5 layers of paper.

Roll heavy paper into 7 cones and fasten them to the piñata with masking tape as shown—5 cones circling the piñata, one pointing out the front, and one pointing out the back. Apply a final layer of colored paper dipped in papier-mâché, making sure to seal the joints.

Allow the piñata to dry completely—a day or two. Cut an opening at the top of the piñata with a sharp knife and punch a hole on either side of the hole with a nail. (NOTE: Illustration is shown without cones so this detail can be seen more easily.)

Fill the piñata with small candies or toys. Loop a heavy string or light rope through the top and hang on a tree branch or basketball hoop, where the piñata can swing freely.

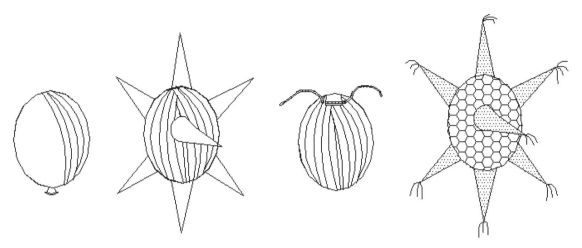

Students take turns being blindfolded and spun (traditionally, 33 times to honor the 33 years that Jesus lived) before trying to hit the piñata with a bat. When the piñata breaks, all students share the treats.

The star-shaped piñata represents the star that guided the wise men to Bethlehem. Each of the seven points represents an important sin, with the body of the piñata representing the devil. When the piñata is broken open, it symbolizes the freeing of the goodies from the devil and the breaking of sin by the bat, which symbolizes Christianity.

A simple alternative to making a papier-mâché piñata is to fill a paper grocery bag with treats, tie the end closed, and hang it. Or, simply purchase a ready-made piñata from the store.

SUGGESTIONS FOR FURTHER ACTIVITIES

History: Research the ancient civilizations that lived in the land that is now Mexico.

History: Research the arrival of Cortez in South America and the Spanish influence in Mexico.

Literacy/Language Arts: Find stories about Christmas, about how Las Posadas is celebrated in Mexico, and about how Christmas is celebrated in other countries around the world.

Language Arts: Have children write a poem, song, or story about Christmas or about Mexico.

Science: Research cactus plants—locate where they grow in the world, what different types of cactus plants look like, and what type of climate they need.

Math: When making bizcochitos, discuss measurement conversions and practice converting fractions and whole numbers and ounces and metric system measurements, using the recipe as a guide. (See the chapter entitled **Measurements and Metric Conversions.**)

SUPPLEMENTAL CHAPTERS

Timelines and Number Lines

As you read, think about how timelines and number lines are similar. How are they different?

TIMELINES

A timeline is a snapshot of history. Cultures keep track of years based on important events. The Hebrew calendar calculates years from the creation of the world, according to scripture. The date of creation is the Hebrew year zero. Muslims track the number of years from their prophet Muhammad's flight from Mecca. On the Muslim calendar, that year is zero. On our calendar, that date was AD 622. Why the difference?

In western culture, we don't track our years based on the creation of the world or on Muhammad. We track our years based on the number of years before or after the birth of Jesus Christ. You may hear years referred to as BC or BCE. BC stands for "before Christ." BCE stands for "before the common era." Both refer to the years before our year zero—before the year Christ was born.

All the years before the year zero count *backward*. The initials BC or BCE are then written *after* the year. For example, we say that 500 years before the birth of Christ was the year 500 BC (or 500 BCE). Of course, people living in 500 BC didn't *know* it was before Christ, because that date had not happened yet.

Similarly, you may hear years labeled AD or CE. AD stands for the Latin phrase *Anno Domini*, which means "in the year of our Lord (Christ)." CE stands for "common era." Both refer to the same years—the years *after* our year zero. These years count *forward* from zero, and the labels AD or CE are written *before* the date. For example, the modern date AD 2010 (or CE 2010) means that the year is 2,010 years past the birth of Christ.

To get a picture of history, we could use a simple timeline, like this:

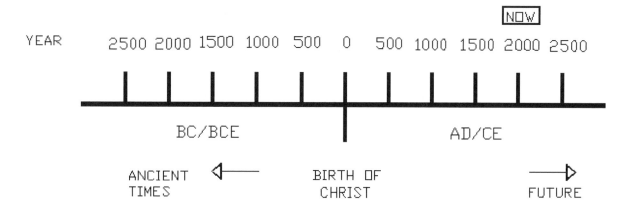

Make Your Own Timeline (Language Arts)

Make a timeline of your life, with your birth as zero. Dates to the left of zero would be events that happened before you were born. Dates to the right of zero would represent your life and things you expect to happen in the future, such as your next birthday and the year you will graduate from high school. What important events would you include on your timeline?

NUMBER LINES

A number line is a visual way to express numbers. Positive numbers are numbers whose value is greater than zero and are written on a number line to the right of zero. Negative numbers are numbers whose value is less than zero and are written to the left of zero on a number line.

How can the value of a number be less than zero? Let's think about money. If you borrow $10.00 from your friend to buy a book, then you owe money you don't have. The amount you "have" is less than zero, because you don't just *not have it*—you *owe* it. On a number line what you owe could be represented as a negative 10.

Pretend you don't owe your friend money. Instead you have $10.00. That $10.00 would be the positive number 10 on a number line. It is money whose value is more than zero.

Now say you owe your friend $10.00, but you find $10.00 in your pocket. After you pay your friend the $10.00 you owe, you have no money left. The amount you have left would be represented as zero (0) on a number line.

Number lines have arrows at each end to show that numbers keep going. Here's how the numbers we discussed would look on a number line:

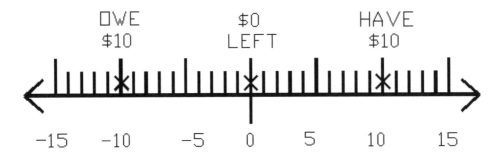

Make a Thermometer Chart (Math, Science)

A thermometer is like a number line. The temperature 32 degrees Fahrenheit (zero degrees Celsius) is the temperature at which water freezes. This temperature could represent zero on a number line. Temperatures colder than 32° Fahrenheit (0° Celsius) represent negative numbers. Temperatures warmer than 32° F (0° C) represent positive numbers.

Draw a number line with 32° F (0° C) at the zero mark. Write degrees below freezing (colder) at the negative (left) end of the number line. Write degrees above freezing (warmer) at the positive (right) end of the number line.

To convert Fahrenheit temperatures into Celsius, subtract 32 from the Fahrenheit temperature to adjust to the Celsius zero. Then multiply the result by 5/9. With C = Celsius and F = Fahrenheit, the equation would look like this:

$$C = 5/9 \ (F - 32)$$

Reverse the equation to convert Celsius to Fahrenheit:

$$F = 9/5 \ (C + 32)$$

Calendars

Many world holidays occur on different dates each year. The dates change because of the calendars people use.

OUR SOLAR CALENDAR

Most of the modern world uses a solar calendar based on the time it takes the earth to circle our sun. But even our calendar of 365 days is not perfectly accurate. It actually takes Earth 365¼ days to circle the sun. But having one 6-hour day each year would be confusing. So instead, our calendar has 365 days a year for three years. Every fourth year we add an extra 24-hour day (February 29). Mathematically, this 24-hour day equals the extra 6 hours per solar year multiplied by 4 years ($6 \times 4 = 24$).

Because our calendar is tied to earth's position around the sun, our seasons begin and end at the same time each year. In other words, our spring always begins in March and our winter always begins in December. But what causes our seasons in the first place? It's not our position around the sun, because the earth generally stays the same distance from the sun as it circles.

The cause of seasons is the earth's tilt. The earth does not spin straight up and down with the North Pole directly above the South Pole. Rather, the earth tilts 23.5 degrees on its axis (the center point on which the earth spins). This tilt determines the number of hours of sunlight that different parts of the earth receive.

When the northern part of the earth where we live (called the northern hemisphere) is tilted toward the sun, it receives sunlight for the longest number of hours each day. The very longest day (about June 22) in the northern hemisphere is called the summer solstice. The shortest day (about December 22, for us) is called the winter solstice. The halfway points between the solstices are called equinoxes. Our spring equinox is about March 21 and our autumnal equinox is about September 22. Think about what the dates for seasons would be for the southern half of the world, and why.

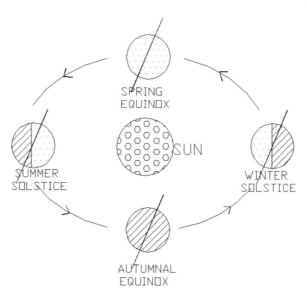

221

LUNAR CALENDARS

Some cultures base their calendars on how the moon appears in our sky. Because the moon swings through space along with the earth, it appears differently during different parts of the month, depending on where the moon, the earth, and the sun are in relation to each other. For example, if the sun is shining directly on the moon, the moon appears to us as a full circle. At other times, we see the moon as a crescent.

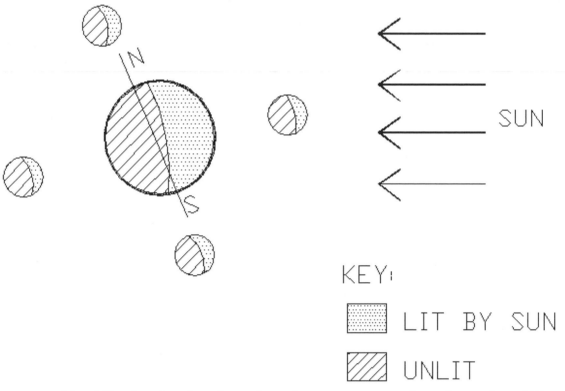

The following drawing shows how the moon appears from the earth at different times of the month. From left to right: new Moon, waning Moon (getting smaller), full Moon, and waxing Moon (getting larger).

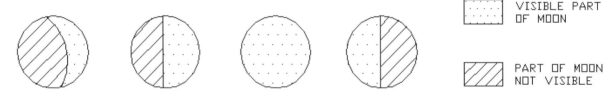

A lunar year is just over 354 days long—almost 11 days shorter than our solar year. The result is that dates and seasons rotate through a lunar calendar over the years. What would it be like to have summer in October one year and in March another year?

The Hebrew lunar calendar adds a thirteenth month seven times during a 19-year period, to catch up with our solar calendar. Whereas our day begins at midnight, the Hebrew day begins at sunset.

The Islamic calendar is calculated in every country based on when certain people see the rising of the new moon. Because the Islamic calendar is 11 days shorter than a solar calendar, Islamic holidays move along our calendar, taking 32½ years to complete a cycle. Like the Hebrew calendar, Islamic days begin at sunset.

There are several 12-month lunar calendars used in India; they add extra days every few years. Hindu calendars are divided into 12 segments based on heavenly bodies, each named for an astrological sign. The Hindu day begins at sunrise.

Ancient China also developed a lunar calendar of 354 days, with an extra month every few years to catch up with the solar calendar. Chinese years are named after animals. Twelve animals represent a cycle of twelve years, after which the cycle repeats. The animals are the rat, ox, tiger, rabbit, dragon, snake, horse, ram, monkey, rooster, dog, and pig. The Chinese day begins at midnight, like ours.

Watching the moon; adding months; horses, monkeys, pigs. . . It makes our own calendar look pretty simple, doesn't it?

Stars of Wonder (Science, Language Arts)

Have you ever noticed that stars appear to move slowly across our sky during the night and over a period of months? Actually, stars stay in the same place. It is our earth that moves in relation to them. A study of stars and their location in the sky was part of many ancient religions. The Hindu religion believes that each person is influenced by the group of stars (called a *constellation*) that was overhead when that person was born. The following Zodiac signs are part of modern astrology.

ZODIAC SIGN CONSTELLATIONS

STAR CONSTELLATION	DATE OF BIRTH	CHARACTER/ OBJECT
Aries	March 21 through April 20	The Ram
Taurus	April 21 through May 21	The Bull
Gemini	May 22 through June 21	The Twins
Cancer	June 22 through July 22	The Crab
Leo	July 23 through August 21	The Lion
Virgo	August 22 through September 23	The Virgin
Libra	September 24 through October 23	The Scales
Scorpio	October 24 through November 22	The Scorpion
Sagittarius	November 23 through December 22	The Archer
Capricorn	December 23 through January 20	The Goat
Aquarius	January 21 through February 19	The Water Carrier
Pisces	February 20 through March 20	The Fishes

See which constellation was over the earth when you were born. Find a star chart online or at the library. See where the constellations are located in the sky and what they look like.

Pretend the star chart contains connect-the-dot pictures. Create new constellations of your own. What shapes can you imagine? Each of the constellations in the astrological Zodiac has characteristics associated with it. Write a story about the constellation you've "discovered."

Latitude and Longitude

One way we locate places on the earth is by latitude and longitude—imaginary lines that divide the earth into sections.

LATITUDE

Imagine slicing a solid ball in half horizontally. That would create two pieces with a flat surface on one end of each. If Earth were that ball, the equator would be like the flat circle. Latitude lines are imaginary lines that are parallel to the equator, as if the earth were sliced into circles, each circle getting smaller toward the poles.

We number latitude lines, starting with zero at the equator, according to the number of degrees north (N) or south (S) of the equator. The number of degrees has to do with the angle of the location in relation to the equator.

Angles? Earth is a ball shape. How can it have angles?

Imagine we can see through the earth. The circle going through the earth at the equator is one plane. That means it has no height or depth, so there is no angle FROM the equator TO the equator. Put a different way, the angle FROM the equator TO the equator is zero.

The angle from the equator to the North Pole, however, is a 90-degree angle. Therefore, the latitude at the North Pole is 90 degrees North. Locations between zero and 90 represent angles relative to the equator.

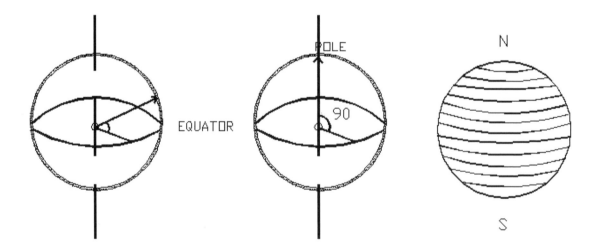

LONGITUDE

Longitude lines also help locate points on the earth. Longitude lines go from pole to pole like strips of an orange peel—wider between them at the equator and narrower towards the poles. Longitudes measure from one point on the earth *around* to another.

The equator goes completely around the earth to form a circle. In mathematics, every circle has 360 degrees that take you from the beginning of the circle, all the way around and back to the beginning. The DISTANCE from one point on that circle to another is expressed as a number of degrees around the circle. For historical reasons, we measure longitude as the number of degrees east (E) or west (W) of the Royal Astronomical Observatory in Greenwich, England.

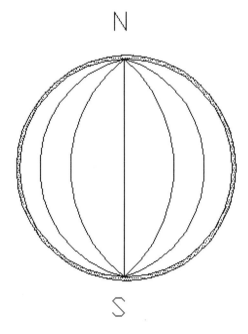

Where in the World Are We? (Math, Geography)

Find out the latitude and longitude of your town by looking it up, or by estimating it on a map. Then switch the N/S latitude and E/W longitude. For example, if your town is located at 40 N latitude and 125 W longitude, check to see what is at 40 S latitude and 125 W longitude. What is at 40 N latitude and 125 E longitude? Then try 40 S latitude and 125 E longitude.

Measurements and Metric Conversions

There are many ways to measure things. We can look at how much space an object occupies, how much it weighs, how long it is, how much area it uses, and how hot or cold it is. Then once we decide *how* we want to measure something, we must decide *what form* of measurement to use.

DO IT YOURSELF

Here are some measurement charts to help you convert standard and metric measurements. Measure various objects in your classroom, using either standard or metric units. Then convert them into the other unit using these charts. Happy measuring!

MEASURING CAPACITY (LIQUID AND DRY MEASUREMENTS)

STANDARD MEASUREMENT	STANDARD CONVERSION	METRIC CONVERSION
1 teaspoon	1/3 tablespoon	5 milliliters
1 tablespoon	3 teaspoons	15 milliliters
1 fluid ounce	2 tablespoons	30 milliliters or 0.03 liter
1 cup	16 tablespoons or 8 fluid ounces	240 milliliters or 0.24 liter
1 pint	2 cups	480 milliliters or 0.47 liter
1 quart	4 cups or 32 fluid ounces	960 milliliters or 0.95 liter
4.2 cups	34 fluid ounces	1 liter or 1000 milliliters
1 gallon	4 quarts or 128 fluid ounces	3.8 liters

MEASURING WEIGHT

STANDARD WEIGHT	METRIC WEIGHT
0.035 ounce or 0.0002 pound	1 gram or 1000 milligrams
1 ounce or 0.06 pound	28 grams
3.5 ounces	100 grams
1 pound or 16 ounces	454 grams or 0.45 kilogram
2.2 pounds	1 kilogram or 1000 grams
2000 pounds or 1 ton	0.9 metric ton
1.1 ton	1 metric ton or 1000 kilograms

MEASURING DISTANCE

STANDARD MEASUREMENT	METRIC MEASUREMENT
0.039 inch	1 millimeter
0.39 inch	1 centimeter or 10 millimeters
1 inch	25 millimeters or 2.54 centimeters or 0.025 meter
1 foot or 12 inches	30 centimeters or 0.3 meter
1 yard or 3 feet or 36 inches	90 centimeters or 0.9 meter
39.37 inches or 3.28 feet or 1.09 yard (1 yard + 3.4 inches)	1 meter or 100 centimeters or 1000 millimeters
0.6 mile	1 kilometer or 1000 meters
1 mile	1609 meters or 1.6 kilometers

MEASURING AREA

STANDARD MEASUREMENT	METRIC MEASUREMENT
0.15 square inch	1 square centimeter
1 square inch	6.45 square centimeters
1 square foot	0.09 square meter
1 square yard	0.83 square meter
1.19 square yard	1 square meter
1 acre or 43,560 square feet or 4840 square yards or	4047 square meters
0.38 square mile	1 square kilometer
1 square mile or 640 acres	2.59 square kilometers

MEASURING TEMPERATURE

To convert temperatures from Fahrenheit to Celsius, use the following formula (F = Fahrenheit; C = Celsius).

5/9 (degrees F − 32) = degrees C

To convert temperature from Celsius to Fahrenheit, reverse the formula.

9/5 (degrees C + 32) = degrees F

Flags

Vexillology [pronounced veks-ih-LOL-uh-jee] is the study of flags. Here are some flag facts.

FLAG SYMBOLISM

Flag colors have special meanings. Red can symbolize blood shed in the fight for freedom. White often means peace. Orange represents courage and sacrifice. Black may represent determination, ethnic heritage, or defeating one's enemies. Blue often represents freedom, justice, or prosperity. Green can symbolize the earth, agriculture, or the Islam religion. Yellow often represents the Sun, wealth, or justice.

Groups of colors also have specific meanings. Many countries have red, white, and blue flags, inspired by the flags adopted by France and the United States after gaining their independence. Many flags of Arab countries use red, white, black, and green to signify their unity. Many African flags use red, yellow, and green to show unity with other African countries.

Flags also may contain symbols important to that country. For example, the 50 stars on the American flag represent the 50 states. The cross on the flags of England, Scotland, and Denmark represents the cross of Jesus Christ.

PARTS OF A FLAG

Isn't a flag just a rectangular piece of fabric with colors and designs? Yes, but each part of the flag has a different name and purpose. When a flag is flown, the flagpole should be to the left of the flag as the person is looking at it. When the flag is hung on a flagpole correctly, the side seen by a person facing it is called the *obverse*, and the other side is called the *reverse*.

Every flag is divided into 4 quarters, called *cantons*. The two left-hand cantons next to the pole are called the *hoist*, because that edge is hoisted (raised) up the pole. The two right-hand cantons away from the pole are called the *fly*, because that edge flies freely in the air.

Not all flags are the same size or shape. Each flag has an official ratio. This means that the proportions of the flag width and length remain the same even if the flag is made larger or smaller. For example, the ratio of narrow Pan-Arabian flags is different from the ratio of the fatter Mexican flag. That way, whether the flags are large or small, the Pan-Arabian flags remain narrower than the Mexican flag.